WHAT'S NEW IN RELIGION?

WHAT'S NEW IN RELIGION?

A Critical Study of New Theology, New Morality
and Secular Christianity

by

KENNETH HAMILTON

WILLIAM B. EERDMANS PUBLISHING COMPANY
GRAND RAPIDS, MICHIGAN

1446332

I am sure no new theology can really be theology, whatever its novelty, unless it express and develop the old faith which made those theologies that are now old the mightiest things of the age when they were new.

— *Peter Taylor Forsyth,* **Positive Preaching and the Modern Mind**

CONTENTS

PART 1: ABOUT THE WORD "NEW"   9
   One: The New and the Pseudo-New   11
   Two: The New and the Old   17

PART 2: ABOUT THE NEW THEMES   25
   Three: The Return of Religion   27
   Four: The Shape of a New Theology   37
   Five: Clearing a Space for Religion   45
   Six: Some God-Hypotheses   52

PART 3: ABOUT BONHOEFFER'S
     "WORLDLY" CHRISTIANITY   65
   Seven: The God Who Is Not a Hypothesis   67
   Eight: Faith and Its Religious Garment   77

PART 4: ABOUT THE SECULAR IN
     FAITH AND MORALS   89
   Nine: The Secular Made Sacred   91
   Ten: New Morality   107

PART 5: HOW TO REGRESS BY WANTING ONLY
     TO PROGRESS, AND HOW TO BE CON-
     TEMPORARY BY NOT BEING AFRAID
     OF THE PAST   125
   Eleven: The Return of Liberalism   127
   Twelve: Liberal and Conservative   140
   Thirteen: Religion and Man's Coming of Age   150
   Fourteen: Both the New and the Old   161
Appendix   172
Bibliography   175
Suggestions for Further Reading   176

Part 1

ABOUT THE WORD "NEW"

ONE

THE NEW AND THE PSEUDO-NEW

"What, and is it really you again?" quoth I:
"I again, what else did you expect?" quoth she.
— *Robert Browning,* Fifine at the Fair

There is a lot of talk these days about a New Morality, a New Theology, and a New Christianity. The word "new" is a good word to hear, suggesting all kinds of pleasant happenings. We make appropriate noises over the neighbors' new baby, somewhere along the scale running between the embarrassed male grunt and the uninhibited female squeal of delight. We convalesce after illness, and thrill to the discovery of new health flowing in. Or we share the lift of spirit that comes when someone is able to cut himself free from a bad situation and make a new start. Yet of course "new" does not necessarily mean the beginning of young life, the influx of fresh energy, and the leaving behind of past mistakes and difficulties. We just tend to think that it does. It refers, in fact, to the latest thing around, which may as well be a death as a birth, a cancer as a cure. Some clear thinking over the use of the word "new" is imperative, considering how it keeps cropping up all over the place.

There can be no doubt that the word "new" is overworked. In advertising, no product seems to be presented to the public without it. If not actually made part of the product's name ("New Blippo"), it is likely to feature in an introductory phrase ("new model," "new formula"). Every effort is made to show that the newness is not yesterday's newness, but a newness belonging to the very latest moment. ("Try the New

11

Improved Electric Toothbrush with the exclusive new feature of Balanced-Touch Power-Steering. You'll never go back to old-style electric toothbrushing.")

The thinking behind this approach is transparent enough, and reasonable enough in its way, too. Since technology fed by scientific research is constantly advancing man's power to *do* and to *make,* the members of a technological society need to be told how the benefits of technological progress are being passed on to them in a concrete, tangible form. Things that we buy (or pay taxes for) embodying the latest know-how are things that permit you and me to share in the power of our society to control the environment. It is not simply a matter of wanting to keep up with the Joneses, although that is encouraged as strenuously as possible in a consumers' society that is run on planned obsolescence. Even without the persuaders (hidden and otherwise) all around us, we could hardly live in the midst of conspicuous productivity and not resent being elbowed out of our place at the table when Mother Technology's pie is being cut. With the smell of fresh baking in the air, last week's leftovers are hardly appetizing.

So we demand our continually restyled automobiles and our participation in the space race; and, if some of us make a gesture of revolt and retire into bearded and sandaled subcultures mimicking the pre-industrial world, we take care to trail our modishly ragged beggar's coats in places where we can count on sizable crumbs falling our way from the rich man's table of our affluent society. If every suburbanite expects his patch of well-mowed lawn, every hippie expects his grass too. A culture that had turned its back on continual technological progress would not have produced millions of color TV sets; but it would not have produced LSD either.

Technology by its very nature is progressive, productive of the new. The new is better than the old, because it is a refinement on the old. We do not use a horse to carry our merchandise or a handle to wind our phonographs once there are more efficient and easier ways to achieve these ends. Natural materials used for a wide variety of purposes are less satisfactory than synthetic materials designed for specific purposes, and men are less quick, exact, and tireless than machines. So we have moved into the age of plastics and of computers. Yet the fact that newness in

12

the realm of technology is the touchstone of excellence does not mean that newness, as such, is good in any other realm. It certainly does not mean that "new" and "good" can be equated universally. The excellence that can be progressively advanced by technical knowledge is in the area of efficiency in devising techniques for harnessing the forces of nature and putting them to work for us. When any other goal comes into the picture, what is newest is far from being what is obviously best. In the realm of art, for example, there is no connection between development in technique and aesthetic excellence. Jackson Pollock is not "better" than Leonardo da Vinci, or Leonardo da Vinci "better" than Giotto. In the realm of politics a new administration is not necessarily an improvement on the old one it replaces, and though statesmen can profit from the mistakes of their predecessors, they do not become progressively wiser on that account. Andrew Johnson is not commonly considered a "better" President than Abraham Lincoln, although he came later. Both realms deal in qualities that are unique, not progressive.

In areas concerned with human beings and living values, as opposed to areas concerned with manipulating things, newness is no obvious recommendation. If anything, it is exactly the opposite. When the bare fact of being new is stressed, there is room for a suspicion that other, more relevant characteristics are being soft-pedaled, and that an attempt is being made to stampede the emotions into welcoming something before the judgment has had time to take a proper look at it. Earlier this century a university professor spoke about a new conception of knowledge that was to replace the traditional notions of academic freedom and the university as a place of unbiased research. The new way which was "coming and becoming" could be seen only by eyes opened by a new courage. Said Martin Heidegger in 1933, summing up his argument,

> The new courage must be conditioned into steadfastness, for the struggle for the educational strongholds of the leaders will take long. It will be fought with the energies of the new state which the people's chancellor Adolf Hitler will bring to reality.

Evidently, there is no easier way of recommending submission to tyranny than by naming it "the new courage" fighting for "the new freedom."

Heidegger's pro-Nazi address is an extreme case. But the principle stands and should make us aware how deceptive the word "new" can be. When applied to things man himself makes, it has some positive content. But applied to human realities, to ideas, ideals, and aspirations found among living people, it is an empty word into which any content whatsoever may be poured. Its capacity to arouse sympathetic emotion, on the other hand, is beyond doubt; for it is a word suggesting hope. Alexander Pope's gift for putting a commonplace into terse memorability was never better displayed than in the familiar couplet from his *Essay on Man,*

> *Hope springs eternal in the human breast;*
> *Man never is, but always to be blessed.*

And the blessed word "new" somehow always succeeds in convincing *homo sapiens* that the felicity that has never yet arrived is coming speedily and will be delivered by the next mail. This is why we are all so easily taken in by the pseudo-new. We warm to the quack whose promises of instant cures are backed by a description of how his "new scientific discoveries" have been ignored by a conservative medical profession unwilling to depart from the old, conventional methods of treatment; or to the "con man" whose scheme for making us immediately rich delights us because it appears to be such a new, brilliant, original suggestion, until we discover it to be the second oldest trick in the world for separating a fool from his money.

Heidegger's "new vision," of course, was neither his nor new nor anything resembling a vision, but a classic example of deception through use of the pseudo-new. His eagerness to turn himself into an echo of Hitler was one more example of the age-old story of intellect submitting to brute power. The story is always particularly depressing on account of the fact that knowledge — especially knowledge of the past — is our best protection against being misled by the pseudo-new. Yet, time and again, the guardians of knowledge have been among the first to hail with enthusiasm the pseudo-new, either because they were unable to identify it or because they were unwilling. Heidegger did not stand alone in the Germany of 1933, where his enthusiasm for the New Order was shared by the sophisticated and the simple alike. Remembering this should make us ponder, not

14

only the emotional appeal of the word "new," but also the conditions contributing to spring the trap of emotion so as to surround the word with an aura of unbounded hope.

Movements bearing the label "New —" are often, in the wisdom of hindsight, seen to be relatively small ripples in the pond of human history. To take a few instances, there was New Art (the *Art Nouveau* movement) towards the close of the nineteenth century, New Thought at the beginning of the twentieth, and the New Look in clothes after the last World War. Now we know very well that art, thought and fashion have all gone through hundreds of much more startling and significant revolutions than the ones dignified with that distinguishing epithet *New*. What the movements had in common was hardly exceptional boldness or originality. They did share another characteristic, however, which had less to do with their intrinsic qualities than with the time when they were born. Each followed a period of relative stagnation and unoriginality — or so it seemed at the time — and each claimed to break radically with tradition and to inaugurate a fresh style. Dash, élan, flair, disdain of old stereotypes — this was the image each sought to impose on the public mind. The now almost forgotten New Look in fashion, for instance, was Europe's sigh of relief over the ending of the shortage imposed by the War. After years of clothes rationing and drab functionalism in military and civilian design it was possible once again to drape extravagant quantities of material over the female frame, so skirts lengthened and sleeves billowed.

A similar confluence of circumstances can be seen in the political field. The New Deal of the Roosevelt era and the New Frontier of the Kennedy administration were rallying cries in the face of a situation where inertia was breeding hopelessness and cynicism; and their success was most evident in the creation of an atmosphere where sections of the nation, at least, were persuaded that optimism was again possible since leadership was not going by default. Hitler's New Germany was created around the myth of the leader embodying the national will, and the myth was nurtured by propaganda to the effect that the Weimar Republic was a period of frustration when the nation lay supine under the injustices imposed by the Treaty of Versailles. If the Third Reich was one New Movement that was no minor disturbance in the ongoing current of history, that was because the Nazi party was able to draw upon forces that were far from new, and to connect itself with old racial memories going far back into the past.

Are New Theology and New Morality also reactions to a feeling of frustration and appeals to rediscover hope in the presence of a vacuum of apathy? In this study I shall try to show that to a large extent they are, and that, to this extent, they fall into a predictable pattern. But there is one more aspect of the appeal of the word "new" to be considered. It is quite a basic one, and perhaps for that reason not too easy to pinpoint successfully. It has to do with the tensions between "new" and "old."

TWO

NEW AGAINST OLD

Ring out the old, ring in the new....
—Alfred, Lord Tennyson, In Memoriam

In every generation there is a running conflict between age and youth, old ways and new ways, tradition and innovation. From the beginning of history the elderly have been heard to grumble that they don't know what the world is coming to nowadays, while the young have gone around mystified by their parents' inability to see that the world has moved on since they themselves were young. The tensions caused by the generation gap are never really resolved. They are just displaced, when the young grow older and discover that they too are being written off as back numbers by the next generation. The rhythm of life continues, carrying its tensions within it.

The rhythm of life, expressing the realities of our biological existence, can never be ignored or defied without serious consequence to ourselves. Our deepest feelings, our greatest insights into the world around us, our capacity for enjoyment and for sympathetic understanding: all these have their roots here, even if they rise to mature on another level. Biological existence is bounded by birth and death, and alternates between growth and decay. Each life in the natural sphere, while being a structured part of the whole, is also unique ... something *new*.

In this sphere the word "new" is an unambiguously happy word, a word of hope without parallel. A new thing produced by technological skill is, strictly speaking, only a novelty. Being the temporary end result of a continuing process, in principle it is already outmoded as soon as it has been put to use. It not only

17

ends on the scrap heap, it is *intended* for the scrap heap. But a new life brings into being that which can never be rendered obsolete — itself. Therefore the small boy was quite right when he replied to the visitor's question, "How old is the baby?" with an indignant, "She's not old at all. She's brand new!" His sister's birth for him was a significant event that had just changed his world. It had brought about a new order in his experience, and it was not to be merged into the background of the old order, the way things used to be.

Of course, the biologically new is from the first moment of existence caught up in the rhythm of life and so has begun to grow old. Yet for personal, as opposed to narrowly biological, existence the limits of life lie between the extremes of *old* and *new* rather than between those of *old* and *young*. Our lives continue to have meaning and purpose just so long as they continue to carry the hopefulness belonging to birth into the ongoing stream of our personal histories. To experience each morning as a new day is to be alive. When we see nothing more than a repetition of the old, tiresome round stretching ahead of us the touch of death is already pressing on our shoulders. This explains why nearly every religion features rites of purification and renewal inviting worshippers to die to the old way of life and rise reborn to the new. Central to the Christian faith in particular is the new birth (John 3) ; the gift of the one who says, "Behold, I make all things new" (Rev. 21:5).

Though all our lives we travel the road leading inexorably from youth to age, the terms "old" and "young" are always very much relative to the place on the road where we happen to be at the moment. The six-year-old knows himself to be really grown up compared with four-year-old "babies." The teenager at times sees himself as a world-weary ancient, with nothing more to experience and with no future beckoning him forward. The fifty-year-old says with conviction, "I don't feel middle-aged," and the eighty-year-old tells the seventy-year-old, "You're still a youngster." All this is not necessarily self-deception. The rhythm of life is more flexible than we have usually imagined, especially with regard to its later years. Social scientists recently have gone far to disprove the popular superstition that you can't teach an old dog new tricks. For that matter, around 400 B.C. the Greek dramatist Sophocles was supposed to have answered the plea of his sons that at ninety he was not competent to handle his affairs by reading to the judges his latest play. So long as one is capable of finding "the new," age is not of first importance. Nevertheless, the rhythm of life makes itself felt universally, though not rigidly. The generation gap remains.

An imaginative expression of the gap is given in William Wordsworth's "Immortality" Ode. There the poet, who responds still to the "innocent brightness of a new-born Day," mourns his inability to respond to the "sweet May-morning" with the spontaneity he once felt in himself and now sees in others who are young — as he no longer is.

> *The Youth who daily farther from the east*
> *Must travel, still is Nature's priest,*
> *And by the vision splendid*
> *Is on his way attended;*
> *At length the Man perceives it die away*
> *And fade into the light of common day.*

What Wordsworth calls the light of common day is the perspective upon life recorded in the first chapter of Ecclesiastes, where human life is no longer at a sweet May morning but has moved on to a chill October evening.

> *What does man gain by all the toil*
> *at which he toils under the sun?*
> *A generation goes, and a generation comes,*
> *but the earth remains for ever.*
> *The sun rises and the sun goes down,*
> *and hastens to the place where it rises.*
> *The wind blows to the south,*
> *and goes round to the north;*
> *round and round goes the wind,*
> *and on its circuits the wind returns.*
> *All streams run to the sea,*
> *but the sea is not full;*
> *to the place where the streams flow,*
> *there they flow again.*
> *All things are full of weariness;*
> *a man cannot utter it;*
> *the eye is not satisfied with seeing,*
> *nor the ear filled with hearing.*
> *What has been will be,*
> *and what has been done is what will be done;*

19

and there is nothing new under the sun.
Is there a thing of which it is said,
  "See, this is new"?
It has been already
  in the ages before us.

(Eccles. 1:3-10)

We may call Ecclesiastes' view of human experience realism or cynicism, as we choose. But we should remember that October is on the calendar as well as May; and, while youth is impressed chiefly with the newness of each event it encounters, age has learned that single events are parts of a larger pattern. "You would think there had never been a baby in the world before," is the perennial comment of the older generation upon the reaction of new parents to their first taste of parenthood. In a sense, of course, there never has been. A unique event has brought a wholly new joy to that particular home. But the structure of life that makes birth one of the commonplaces of nature is equally important to remember. And it is the non-novel, repeatable pattern of life's fabric that chiefly impresses itself upon us as we grow older. The more we become anxious to find out what things are in themselves, rather than viewing them always through our own private interest in them, the more we establish our humanity. To love truth, accepting the world as it is and not expecting it to conform to our wishes or to flatter our ego: this is to advance to maturity as members of the human race. We have to learn to walk in the light of common day, however dreary that may seem at times, because we have no justification for demanding exemption from the common lot and no excuse for evading whatever the hard, unflattering daylight may disclose.

The passage from the vision of youth, centered on its imaginative reaction to life, and the matter-of-factness of maturity are characterized by the experience of disillusionment. However necessary the experience may be, it is a traumatic one, bringing complex reactions. Cynicism and a debilitating world-weariness are likely to follow a violent swing from the first to the second, if there is no second birth of the spirit to restore inward resources and to counter the depressing effect of disappointed hopes. Ex-revolutionaries make the most entrenched reactionaries! On the other hand, the reaction of youth's impatience against those who

20

insist that its visions of a better world are unrealistic and immature has the effect of turning the generation gap into a battle front. What ought to be a cooperative effort, joining hope to realism, usually becomes a bitter fight, seen from one side as a struggle of the new and good against the old and evil, and from the other as irresponsibility pitted against wisdom.

If the distance between youth and age were a rigid affair, tied to the calendar-chart of life instead of being the flexible thing it is, the struggle between new and old at any one time would be relatively easy to diagnose and resolve. In fact, the interaction of age groups usually is very hard to make sense of. The expected divisions are almost always blurred. In such an era as ours, where youth is an expanding section of the population and is self-conscious about itself as a group, it is to be expected that the gulf between the thinking of those turned towards the new and those clinging to the old will be accented ("Never trust anyone over thirty"). But it frequently happens that those most concerned to climb aboard every passing bandwagon — or to construct one of their own and invite youth to join in — are the middle-aged. They wish to prove that they are not on the wrong side of the gulf that separates the revolutionaries from the reactionaries. The current cliché, "traditional concepts are no longer relevant to the contemporary situation," seems to be an especial favorite of the over-forties.

It is interesting to recall that in the fable of the emperor's new clothes the truth about the emperor's nakedness was blurted out by a small child. He was untroubled by doubts as to whether the traditional concept of clothes had relevance to the contemporary situation, while the adults around him were afraid not to appear thoroughly up-to-date.

As each generation rebels against the values and attitudes of the previous one, the historian of culture who tries to see the larger picture beyond the immediate clash of "new" and "old" is likely to view the successive rebellions as so many swings of the pendulum. What is called new not only has been already in the ages before but very frequently has been in the generation immediately preceding the last one. Just as we walk by the spring of the stride that leaves the foot to the rear which was previously out in front, so we progress by an alternation of visions whereby ideas only yesterday declared to be "out" and hopelessly old-fashioned return again as the "in" thing. One fascinating aspect of the present furor over the New Theology is the way in which some of the champions of the "radical" theology of thirty years ago are finding a new audience for their unchanged ideas and are displaying a youthful exuberance as they plunge into a second bout of their old battle.

Today all kinds of experts and nonexperts join in haranguing us about how the changes going on around us in every department of life are so rapid and so extensive that we are in a unique situation, one never experienced before in the ongoing story of mankind and one in which the past gives us no guidance. The fact of rapidly accelerating change resulting from the development of modern technology with the drastic disruption of social organization and traditional ways of thought entailed in this development is real enough. That we are all confused and disconcerted by the speed with which we are being pulled into the "new" world — whether we claim to like or loathe what is happening around us — is also patent. But the pretense that we are in a totally new situation, in which the past has no lesson to teach us, looks suspiciously like a fresh form of an old myth: the myth of the phoenix that finds renewed youth again only after it has been totally reduced to ashes. As a myth, the phoenix-picture is useful, even necessary. Every generation thinks of itself as the vanguard of a new humanity freed from the guilt and shame of the past; and, if it fails to keep its vision, it loses its nerve and collapses into cynical apathy. But as a literal statement about the actual world we live in it is nonsense, wicked nonsense that encourages the worst of illusions. We cannot continue to exist without carrying with us our memories, both individual and collective. The past goes with us every step of the way, and the more resolutely we seek the new future, the more we become aware of the present power of the old past — a fact that is being graphically illustrated at the moment by the internal problems of the new nations of Africa.

Meanwhile, under the noisy slogan-shouting of self-appointed prophets, contemporary man is behaving in highly predictable ways, and showing all the signs of being just what he always has been in every age: more man than contemporary. Whether he is off to the moon or to the local love-in, the new man of our "unprecedented" times gives no evidence of being about to prove

Ecclesiastes wrong. Parted from his gadgetry and jargon he is still Shakespeare's "poor, bare, forked animal" or Pascal's "reed, the weakest thing in nature."

Happily, he is also still, as Pascal said, "a thinking reed." Though involved willy-nilly in the rhythm of life, none of us has to remain tied entirely to the outlook of his generation, or of any generation. All of us have the ability to rise above reacting automatically and uncritically in favor of the new or in favor of the old. Whether we decide to put this ability to work depends upon whether we value sufficiently the exercise of free intelligence, to prefer independence in judgment to a reputation for being "thoroughly contemporary" (or, alternatively, "a sound man, not mixed up in these modern fads"). In the rhythm of life across the generations, there are times when conservatism tends to stifle new life, and times when the new is passionately championed against the old. During any of the latter phases "mere logic" and "involved argument" hold little appeal to those who feel that now is the time to throw oneself with abandon on the surge of the great wave that is moving on into the future. Yet this is precisely when critical common sense is most needed in order to separate the new from the pseudo-new.

A New Theology! A New Morality! A New Christianity! The present enthusiasm for such titles seems to indicate that the trend for setting the new against the old has declared itself and has begun to gather momentum. Before jumping in with any heated *pro* or *con* argument, however, it might be wise to try to take a look at the situation in which the demand for this trio of "new's" has declared itself. Any individual estimate of the situation will be partial and questionable, yet it is bound to be better than none at all, and better than the kind of vague prophecy which declares, "It is possible that we stand on the brink of a big breakthrough in theology." If we are going anywhere, in what direction are we headed? Surely that is the question that should be asked first of all. To suggest a possible answer is the purpose of my next chapter.

Part 2

ABOUT THE NEW THEMES

THREE

THE RETURN OF RELIGION

To be at all is to be religious more or less.
— *Samuel Butler,* Notebooks

It has become commonplace for magazines that hardly ever gave space to religion previously to publish articles discussing how we ought to think about God, or whether the Ten Commandments are still relevant to a generation with the Pill, or what Bishop Pike has been saying during the past week. Even the word *theology* — not so long ago a word almost as generally unfamiliar as *alchemy* — is now bandied about on all sorts of occasions, and no apologies given.

Evidently the news has got around that the kind of discussion presently going on among the professionals and academicians in the religious field is not just about the type of question that always used to agitate the representatives of the various denominational bodies. Instead, the ground has shifted and the pace has quickened.

The stately old ecclesiastical institutions, to be sure, have not altered their minds or their dispositions to any alarming extent. They are still largely preoccupied with their internal domestic affairs, with (so to speak) the knitting, the diet-sheets, the repainting of the living-room and other day-to-day concerns proper to the upkeep of orderly establishments. Protestants — though not quite all of them — are eager to quote William Temple (who died in 1944) about the ecumenical movement's being the great new fact of our time. But their progress in matters of Church union is the reverse of rapid. The Roman Church, after its spectacular and newsmaking spate of self-criticism and promise of reform at Vatican II, is now applying the brakes under the guidance of a pontiff seemingly anxious above all to prevent a runaway break from established traditions. At the same time, if the spirit of Bourbonism — learning nothing and forgetting nothing — lives on in organized Christianity, there are large and vocal minorities in both the Protestant and the Catholic camps who are not willing to keep step in the denominational procession or to move at the speed set by the majority. To some extent, indeed, they are forcing the pace to quicken. They have attracted a good deal of sympathetic interest on the outside while puncturing much complacent apathy on the inside.

So the winds of change are blowing even in the churches as they are in all other areas of today's world. And not a moment too soon, most of us would say. There are obviously real hopes of a vital renewal within the Christian community in our generation. Yet perhaps what we are seeing is not precisely a rebirth of Christianity, although we may be correct in believing that we are seeing that too. Most of the evidence, at least as I try to read it for what it presents, points to something happening that must affect Christian faith very intimately, but does not primarily have to do with Christian faith.

What we are seeing, I believe, is the return of religion to our culture.

Call it, if you will, a turning of mid-century, rootless Western man to try to find what he has lost: a religious outlook to give him meaning, direction, and purpose in his attempt to cope with his total environment, and to achieve satisfaction from the struggle. And it does not in the least follow that the religious outlook he is seeking is a Christian one. Quite the reverse, in fact; for it is dissatisfaction with the traditional message of Christianity that has left him feeling lost and impels him to a new religious quest. Because Christianity has such deep roots in our Western civilization, it is difficult for most of us to think of reviving religion in our midst in any other way than that of "rediscovering" Christianity. So it is natural that we should be hearing just now a good deal about a New Christianity. But most of the protagonists of a New Christianity make a point of stressing that the faith they envisage for the future will be completely different from everything that has been called "Christian" in the past. Any real continuity between the "Christianity" that is to be (as they hope) and "original" Christianity (which they say they wish to recover) must therefore be judged at best doubtful and problematic. What is not doubtful is the wish to put back into circulation a religious faith that will do for our generation and our culture what religion has done for other generations and other cultures.

There are immediate objections that will be offered to the suggestions that today's return to religion represents a turning-away from Christian faith rather than its rediscovery, and that the "ferment in the Church" is caused in part by those who wish to abolish the Christian message and not wholly by those who wish to renew it. I shall try to meet a couple of these objections briefly in the present chapter, and fill out the picture in succeeding chapters. But first I must explain what I mean by saying that Western man is trying to find the religious outlook he has lost.

Of course, to speak of "mid-century Western man" is a misleading generalization. There is no such thing, although we hear much these days about what contemporary man thinks, or what contemporary man has outgrown, or what contemporary man finds meaningless — as though there were in each age of history some mass-produced model-man of unvarying pattern coming off an assembly-line owned and operated by the spirit of the age. Men are not products to be fitted into identical containers, and they do not all think in the same way in any generation just because they happen to live at the same time. They are, all the same, equally subject to cultural pressures that influence them more than they know. Looking back to other times we can see characteristic patterns of thought and behavior of which the people living then were largely unaware. But how can we know how we ourselves look, lacking as we do the perspective for an impartial viewpoint? We are too near to ourselves and our world to do much more than make inspired guesses. We may collect any amount of data, yet for lack of a proper frame of reference miss their significance entirely. In actual practice we are dependent for our estimate of modern man upon *some* modern men who set themselves up as spokesmen for the rest of us. If their findings articulate what we too have dimly sensed, so that their interpretation of the situation seems to find an echo in our own consciousness, then we must be grateful for the insight they have helped us to achieve. They have allowed us to glimpse, as it were, the contemporary man who lives in each of us.

This procedure may be risky and unreliable, but it helps us to understand better who we are and where we are going. The chief danger is that we shall accept personal judgments as oracular utterances, forgetting that, however shrewd and knowledgeable they may be, they can claim no finality. We must bear in mind always that the interpreters of the contemporary situation read one another and quote one another. Not infrequently, therefore, we accept an interpretation less on account of its merits than on account of our having heard it so many times and in so many places that it imposes itself on us with a spurious authority. Thus hypotheses of uncertain worth but high quotability gain prestige through exposure, and soon are received as dogmas; only to be ousted in favor of some newer dogma as quickly as another easy-to-take phrase becomes popular. In this connection, there is particular relevance in Robert Louis Stevenson's gibe, "Man is a creature who lives not upon bread alone, but principally by catchwords."

Judged by the phrase-test it is easy to describe contemporary man. Not long ago he was busy making friends and influencing people, being resolved to stay alive all his life. But then he went out on the boundary, encountered the absurd, chose authentic existence, recovered the depth-dimension, and recognized an ultimate concern. At the present moment he is willing the death of God, celebrating the secular city, and discovering that the medium is both the message and the massage. This is the man whom Dietrich Bonhoeffer declared to have come of age, able at last to stand on his own feet without the prop of religion. The prevailing dogma among those who claim to stand in Bonhoeffer's line of forward-looking theology is that today's man, if he is capable of entertaining any faith at all, must be contemplating a religionless Christianity capable of being received by a completely secularized society. To doubt this dogma is rank heresy where catchword-orthodoxy reigns.

Bonhoeffer was an exceptionally sensitive observer of the world of his day. Nevertheless, I cannot think that the prevailing fashion of using some of his phrases (especially out of the con-

text of his total faith) as the final word on our present situation
is anything less than totally misleading.

To begin with, the world he described was the world of
disintegrating liberal hopes and expanding totalitarian terrors.
The Church that he knew was a powerless remnant. He could
not think that ever again it would become a cultural, accommodating Church, at home in the world and accepting the role
that the world expected it to play. In his last writings, collected
in *Letters and Papers from Prison,* he anticipated a complete
disappearance of men's trust in the power of religion to give them
peace of mind or the kind of personal adjustment to life that
psychotherapy could now achieve for them. When they ceased
to look to religion to solve their problems for them, to reconcile
them to life's trials, and to give them assurance that they lived
in a snug universe where God existed in order to remove their
sense of guilt, then there would be "a clearing of the decks for
the God of the Bible." He never envisaged the style of life that
was to come after the war — for instance, the "religious revival"
in North America during the fifties. That revival, accompanied
by an unprecedented boom in church building, followed exactly
the pattern of life that he believed had gone for ever. Man-come-
of-age was showing his continued trust in religion to assist him
in achieving the "good life" as reflected in the ideals of contemporary culture. The congregations who filled the comfortable
commodious buildings — many of them reflecting the most ad-
mired contemporary taste — evidently considered a proper regard
for religion to be the crowning glory of the American way of life,
the conclusive evidence that their cultural existence was worthy
of approval by God and man.

Well, the churchly fifties have been followed by the secular
sixties. Much of the inspiration for this change stemmed from
a desire to make modern Christianity less cultural and more
authentically Christian. Some of the emphases of this movement,
especially the desire for a Servant Church, were in line with
Bonhoeffer's thinking. Such books as Peter Berger's *The Noise
of Solemn Assemblies* and Pierre Berton's *The Comfortable Pew*
castigated alike the leaders and the followers of a Church
absorbed in running an inward-looking institution that seemed
to have chiefly a decorative function in society. In *A Public and
a Private Faith* William Stringfellow gave an American version

of Bonhoeffer's protest against an ecclesiasticism content to remain on the borders of life, ministering to individual "spiritual" needs and condemning peripheral vices in the body politic, while avoiding involvement with the power structures and ideologies that were the determining forces in the total community.

Bonhoeffer's own words were increasingly quoted; and the example of his life and death specifically held out as an example, as the ideal of a Christianity involved in the world instead of hiding away from it in a churchly "ghetto," gained popular currency. At the same time his unrealized plans for undertaking a "reinterpretation of biblical concepts" for modern existence challenged the exponents of a Bonhoefferian "worldly" Christianity to attempt what he had not been given time to carry through. It was here, in my opinion, that the movement was largely turned in quite a different direction and transformed, by a shift of emphasis, into its opposite. The New Testament picture of the Christian in the world without being conformed to the world — a picture so vividly present to Bonhoeffer — was forgotten in the enthusiastically entertained vision of a Church lifted out of irrelevance to become a force that the world must reckon with because it spoke to the world's condition. In the area of doctrine this was taken to mean that traditional beliefs were to be updated and brought into line with contemporary world-views; in the area of ethics, that moral problems were to be solved by an appeal to the contemporary conscience; and in general, that the ecclesiastical as such was to disappear as it flowed into the ongoing life of secular society.

The various developments of this vision of Christianity-reinterpreted-for-our-age require separate investigation. The chapters following attempt an appraisal of the characteristics of some of the most prominent among these, and suggest how they stand in relation to one another. At this point it is only necessary to note how easy it is to make the transition from reinterpretation to substitution, from making intelligible to making acceptable through accommodation. The principal reason Bonhoeffer desired a "non-religious" Christianity was the prevalent belief that religion existed to solve personal problems. Those who had turned their back upon religion did so under the impression (rightly, so Bonhoeffer thought) that modern man could solve his own problems without asking the God of religion for help.

When the accent is laid, as it is so commonly now, on the need for making Christianity relevant to today's tasks and to the questions that contemporary man is asking, it is likely that the new interpretation of Christianity that will emerge will be not in the least a "religionless" or "worldly" Christianity, but a worldly religion geared to solve the special type of problem that arises in a secular culture. It may be correct that man "come of age" is not necessarily further from Christian truth when he has turned away from the religious preoccupations of the past to a new trust in his own powers to transform the world and live in it creatively, but the unwarranted conclusion should not be made that, as secular man, he is nearer to Christian obedience than before. If God willed man to come of age, it does not follow that to help man be more wholeheartedly secular must be the Christian's prime duty. Indeed, the call we are hearing directed to the Christian to help to build well the "secular city" sounds altogether too much like a *religious* summons. And it contains little of Bonhoeffer's recognition of the understanding that, while modern man may be asked to "live without God," he is always to live "before God." There is so little evidence that proposed reconstructions of Christianity have left behind problem-solving that we find the reality of God becoming an increasing "problem." The *problem of God* is a phrase increasingly common, even though some claim to have solved the problem by assuring us that the one thing needful for us to know is that God is dead.

The supposition that man-come-of-age is much more concerned with religion than he has been given credit for being lights up ground that is otherwise obscure. Bonhoeffer rightly insisted that religious man, *homo religiosus,* is not at all the same as Christian man. From a Christian standpoint, God-forgetfulness is a less permanent danger than the worship of false gods. The human mind, said Calvin, is a productive factory of idols; and there is no reason to think that it has ceased to be so in the twentieth century, or that henceforth Western man has only two live options: Christianity and unbelief.

We might look at the question of modern man and religion in the following way. Because of the religious mold in which our culture was formed, Christianity has been the sole expression of religion familiar to Western man. With the rise of secular society, religion seemed to be on its way out, a failing force doomed to ultimate extinction — though much more tenacious in its hold upon the imaginations of large sections of the population than most nineteenth-century rationalists thought it to be. After World War II our Western world was in a mood to reconsider the value of religion in its culture. It seemed reasonable to do so; for, while old-fashioned atheists had blamed religion for keeping mankind so long in the Dark Ages and prophesied a future of increasing freedom and worldwide brotherhood of man when religious superstition was left behind, the twentieth century had twice already been plunged into destructive wars and had recently seen tyrannies spring up that had brought back the evils of the Dark Ages, made more deadly through the development of technological know-how.

In the face of this, religion, which promised to solve man's deepest problems — problems that enlightenment and technology had left untouched — might be tried again. And so in the fifties many turned back to the ancestral religion of Christianity. Perhaps traditional religion, after all, could be made to serve the turn. But the familiar pattern of Christianity, even when updated superficially (modern church architecture, union of some church groups, liturgical reform, etc.) did not fill the bill. So the next step was to attempt to update the content of religious belief, urging *radical* reform, a *New* Christianity. Perhaps what was wrong was not religion as such, but the kind of religion. Perhaps this subdivision of religion, Christianity, was too parochial, too exclusive, too tied to its historic past, and too saddled with archaic encumbrances (its scripture, its creed, its priesthoods and ministries) to serve contemporary needs.

Of course, nobody sits down and says, "We need a new religion, let's set about inventing one." (Auguste Comte tried in the nineteenth century, but he remained the only convert to his new faith.) And few of the self-styled radical Christians say in so many words that they want a religion but not Christian faith; though some make clear that for them the decisive factor is the present religious temper of society that demands a complete break with the Christian past.

All this is not to deny that the blowing of the winds of change has brought fresh hopes for a genuine rekindling of Christian faith, or that new and constructive thinking is going on from the side of those whose concern is to present the Christian message,

34

stripped of inessentials and cultural accretions, in a form adapted to the present age. What I am sure has to be said just now is that those who see a New Reformation right at hand (if only supporters of the *status quo* can be prevented from delaying it) are being naive to the point of foolishness. On the other hand, those who see some good changes coming along, while other changes seem incomprehensible and gratuitously offensive, may have a more balanced approach, but they have not grasped the key to the situation.

In our generation, as in all generations, there are antithetical forces at work both in those who work for change and those who work against it. All the winds of change blowing around us do not represent the breath of the Spirit of God. Any of them may equally well have their source in what the New Testament calls the spirit of the world. Similarly, while there are many who fear the challenge to rise to new life and are ready to quench the Spirit rather than be disturbed, there are many also who believe in testing "the spirits to see whether they are from God," since there are many prophets who are falsely inspired (1 John 4:1). The question is not whether a New Christianity is needed today. It is always needed, because a living faith cannot return to yesterday's vision and will not be nourished by manna gathered and kept over until the next day. The question is whether a New Christianity developed expressly to satisfy what we feel to be our needs can be anything except "another gospel," which is welcome because it has the appearance of novelty yet makes no new demands on us, and especially does not threaten to disturb our old image of ourselves. Thus the alternatives facing us are not those of striving for a new understanding of Christianity or of clinging to old forms, of choosing between the risk of facing the future beyond the known and the familiar or of choosing to play it safe and stay put. The alternatives lie between risking the way of Christian faith calling us to be new men and sheltering ourselves in a religion flattering to the Old Adam. We may avoid the risk of faith equally either by clinging to old formulas that have no life in them or by building new structures of theory and practice that, throwing out the "scandal" of the gospel, set up the spirit of the age to be adored with divine honors.

It is tempting to turn aside here to investigate the methods by which the Old Adam, every time he changes his clothes, tries to pass himself off as the type of the New Man. But that must wait until we have looked in more detail at the complex phenomenon of the New Christianity. So first we must give our attention to the New Theology.

FOUR

THE SHAPE OF A NEW THEOLOGY

I own I like a definite form in what my eyes
are to rest upon.
— *Robert Louis Stevenson,* Travels with a Donkey

During the past four or five years there has been a proliferation of books with such titles as *The Honest To God Debate; Guide to the Debate about God; The Death of God Debate; The Secular City Debate;* and so on. The fact that these titles indicate more than a single focus of discussion underlines the current ferment in religious thinking.

No one, definite issue has as yet arisen and asserted itself as *the* issue to which all others are demonstrably subordinate, drawn into its orbit like planets circling a sun. Some have suggested that the "problem of God" has emerged as the central problem to be solved before any further headway can be made in putting order into the prevailing chaos. If this is so, it is not immediately apparent. First of all, there is the thorny question of how one can possibly begin to approach "the problem of God" when some insist that there is only one option open today, namely, to agree that God is dead. In addition, some of the advocates of secular Christianity complicate matters by suggesting that how we are to think about God (if at all) is not important. It is a subject that can wait until a solution presents itself, as it undoubtedly will after a while, out of the practical style of living-in-the-world that we can adopt right now without stopping to solve purely theoretical questions. Dropping that approach, we may ask whether the advent of a New Theology should merit first attention. Then what are we to say about the demands being made for a New Christianity? Surely it is necessary to know what the faith is that we are to take as our starting-point before we contemplate working out a theology for that faith!

Another aspect of the case confronts us when we consider how very little headway most of the "debates" seem to have made in approaching any agreed conclusions. By and large, the debates have consisted of head-on conflicts. Positions have been stated on the one hand and declared to be untenable on the other, with a few mediators suggesting that perhaps there is much to be said on both sides. Advance towards common agreement, as well as progressive clarification of the issues, has been minimal. Not that there has been any lack of good descriptive accounts given. If we want to know just what the particular program of any of the "new" thinkers is, we do not have to look far to find a tolerably accurate picture of it set down for our enlightenment. The difficulty is getting any farther than that. One book in the "debate" class has been hopefully entitled *Radical Theology: Phase Two.* Yet, on examination, this book also turns out to be, for the greater part, *first* reactions to — and often total rejections of — the theology mentioned in the title. So it is not even a matter of the reader's thinking "This is where we came in." We do not seem to have got past the doorway or to have found a place to sit down.

It might look like a useless quest, therefore, to set out to identify a theology which is so protean as to manifest itself in incompatible forms, and which has not made up its mind what it is a theology of. Nevertheless the quest must be embarked upon, unless we are prepared simply to fold our hands and wait for the next new theological rabbit to pop out of the hat, in the hope that this latest phenomenon will give us the clue to all that has gone before. Indeed, that course may well prove to be fruitless, for we have not the slightest guarantee that additional theological programs or calls to yet another religious adventure will do anything to make sense of those we already know; they are far more likely to add still more coals to the fire of confusion. While it is certain that a rapidly changing religious situation will continue to change, making any survey of the field out of date before it has been half-begun, this does not mean that it is useless to look for a pattern in the apparent chaos. I have already suggested that the present situation is at least partly explicable in terms of the search for a religion answering the needs felt in contemporary society, needs that do not seem to be met by traditional Christianity. This is hardly an earth-shattering conclusion, on the face of it. Yet I believe that the implications contained in it may go a long way to explaining the widely diverse "movements" that have been springing up around us. Although there is no single, unified New Theology, there may be visible, among the various elements evident in the ferment in religious thinking, a recognizably new theological shape.

Perhaps we should start looking for a pattern by beginning with what seems most singular and least easy to fit into any pattern.

No aspect of the present ferment has attracted quite so much attention as the "Christian atheism" connected principally with the names of William Hamilton and Thomas Altizer. After all, in a religious context it would be difficult to dream up any pronouncement with greater potential shock-value than the three monosyllables, *"God is dead."* Also sufficiently paradoxical is the suggestion that to deny the present reality of God is the means to establish Christian faith today and not to undermine it. Such a position would seem to merit the title of "radical theology" that this self-styled Christian atheism claimed for itself (cf. Altizer and Hamilton's *Radical Theology and the Death of God*).

The death-of-God theology appeared to come to many people, even professional theologians, as a bolt out of the blue. The effect it gave — especially since it was quickly publicized in popular magazines — was rather as though a householder had answered a ring at the door and found waiting on the doorstep the foreman of a wrecking crew with orders in his hand for the immediate demolition of the home. The protests that followed the news that there were theologians who believed that God was dead resembled the reactions that the householder would have displayed had he heard for the first time, when confronted with the demolition order, that the continued existence of his house was threatened. Yet, at the very least, those who were shocked to find that there were theologians who professed disbelief in God should have heard that the Christian house had been the subject of much discussion for a long time.

39

Some had declared that it badly needed redecoration, some wanted major alterations made, and not a few doubted whether the whole edifice, as it now was, could stand much longer.

The discussion, indeed, had been going on almost as long as anyone could remember. But it gained a fresh impetus and broke into public consciousness in a rather spectacular way with the appearance in 1963 of John Robinson's *Honest To God*. The odd thing was that that little book did not, on the face of it, carry any charge of high explosives.

Bishop Robinson himself has put on record how amazed he was by the immediate and enthusiastic reaction to *Honest To God*. Many knowledgeable commentators since have echoed his amazement, pointing out how little in it was novel or surprising or uniquely iconoclastic, and adding that the line of argument was at many points far from being either convincing or consistent. For his leading ideas Robinson had gone to three already famous theologians: Dietrich Bonhoeffer, Rudolf Bultmann, and Paul Tillich. He had made no pretense of hiding his sources — quite the reverse. What was his own was the conclusion he drew from these thinkers and others of a younger generation who were exploring the same territory. He was sure a new era had arrived in which a crisis in communication was calling for a drastic revision in the way Christianity was presented to the world at large. The terms in which Christian belief was at present being expressed misled those inside the Church and were unintelligible to those outside.

Robinson can be faulted for putting forward an inadequate and even perverse account of traditional theology and for giving the erroneous impression that Bonhoeffer, Bultmann, and Tillich could be made to lie down amicably in the same bed. Yet the effect, however unjustifiable in terms of cold logic, was to make the business of theology seem of practical interest and the updating of Christian thought a possible project. *Honest To God*'s opening chapter, headed "Reluctant Revolution," was the key to the book's impact. Its author left many points in doubt (including the extent of his quarrel with traditional Christian thinking), but he came across with the message that whatever of tradition he decided to jettison or retain was to be his own decision, based upon his independent judgment as

40

a modern man unhindered by the weight of authorities from the past.

Robinson's position was soon labelled soft radicalism by William Hamilton, in contrast with the "hard radicalism" of the Christian atheist's proclamation of the death of God. Nevertheless, in spite of this effort to present his position as a halfway house to a genuinely radical revision of traditional faith, Robinson's initiative was decisive in a way that Christian atheism was not. It opened the road for a whole series of manifestos announcing a New Christianity, of which Christian atheism was only one example. Although Robinson himself has recently declared that he does not believe in any New Theology other than the recasting and updating of the historic Christian message that is the continuing task laid upon the Church in every age, yet the notion of a New Theology was precisely what the appearance of *Honest To God* set in motion. Soon Robinson's disciples-at-a-distance were using the term freely, and joining it to "The New Morality" — also the title of one of *Honest To God*'s chapters. When journalist Ved Mehta of *The New Yorker* magazine went out to find the reason for all the recent hubbub in the ecclesiastical camp, he started from the excitement touched off by *Honest To God*. He called his published report *The New Theologian*.

Once the cry of "New!" has been raised and has found a response, the emotional stresses latent in the generation gap lie ready to be exploited. Immediately the New is opposed to the Old, and the New does not have to justify itself, or even to identify itself precisely. It is already justified because, bathed in the aura of the Living Present, it declares itself victor over the Dead Past. And specific identification is of small importance; for who would dare tie the emerging form of New Life to prescribed limits? The power of the New lies preeminently in its ability to burst the old molds and confound the old categories. Even to question the credentials of the New is to lay oneself open to the charge of being a prisoner of the past, unable to face the challenge of thinking in fresh terms about the hitherto unexperienced.

The failure of "hard radicalism" to take over from its "soft" precursor and to establish itself as *the* form of the New in religious thinking is an illustration of how an attempt to pin

41

down the shape of the New may be self-defeating. For a time it seemed that the phrase "God is dead," which was memorable in the extreme and made a useful slogan to catch the public ear, might become a rallying point for the various streams of "progressive" theologies. But this did not happen. Though the slogan was attention-claiming, it was an extremely difficult one to explain in terms that more than a few academically minded persons could connect with their experience. Then, the initial success of the slogan simply hastened the dissolution of a movement that had never had any intrinsic cohesion. Once people began to ask what *exactly* was meant by the death of God, it was plain that the rallying point could not be broadened out to make a comprehensive party platform. The explanations given revealed widely different opinions both about the "atheism" that was to follow the recognition of the death of God and about the "Christian" quality supposed to emerge out of the resultant godless condition. Radical theology might be expected to be theology on the move. But this radicalism, like Stephen Leacock's celebrated horseman, seemed to be racing madly off in all directions.

Christian atheism is still an ingredient in the stew cooking on the religious stove in the mid-century kitchen. But it is no more than one ingredient. The question of how Christianity is to be related to our modern secular society has come to the forefront of the issues being most urgently debated. So, if one problem is how the New Christian is to understand his relation with God (if indeed the old concept of God can continue to have meaning for him), another problem is how the Church is to understand its place in the world (if indeed the old concept of the Church as something apart from the world can continue to be a meaningful concept). Then there is the problem of how the New Christian is to behave in the modern situation where he finds himself, a problem that has called forth a New Morality in the shape of "situation ethics."

It might seem, then, that New Theology as a movement simply falls apart into separate questions, each one demanding to be considered on its own. Yet perhaps discerning the overall shape of the movement is chiefly a matter of looking below the surface appearances. Some indication of this emerges out of James A. Pike's *A Time for Christian Candor* (1964).

The title of Pike's book is transparently an echo of *Honest To God,* and indeed Ved Mehta writes in *The New Theologian* that Bishop Pike "sounded like an instructor in a department of which Robinson was the head" (p. 25). Pike opens *A Time for Christian Candor* by announcing boldly, "We are in the middle of a theological revolution" (p. 7). He closes with a few suggestions of present beliefs and practices in the Church requiring (1) *Abolition* or (2) *Salvaging* or (3) *Preservation intact, with interpretation.* He wishes, for example, to abolish all ceremonies "which have no meaning to communicate" (p. 137), and to preserve with interpretation "many of the customary externals of worship, which can be beautiful and meaningful in our time" provided "they are not viewed as absolutes" (p. 139). These are rather small mice to be born out of the travail of the theological mountain. Not every revolution looks as tame as this one, or spills so little blood. Or is there more here than is seen?

Pike is anxious to remind us that his very moderate views have drawn the wrath of those who stand for the Old Order in the Church, anxious in fact to the point of calling his recent book *If This Be Heresy* (1967). To play off the Old against the New is certainly (to borrow the language of Stephen Potter's *Gamesmanship*) Pike's ploy. But, granted these tactics, the question still remains as to whether there is really anything solid to play off, or whether the whole thing — accusations of heresy and all — is nothing more than a storm in a teacup.

Pike's revisions of the Old Order that are to prepare the way for the New seem slight enough. Some candles are to be snuffed out, or explanations given as to why they are lit in the first place. Doctrines are to be understood as provisional statements, though not denied so long as they are "meaningful," and the essential truths they embody are to be faithfully recognized and honored. God is not to be pictured in spatial terms but understood as ultimate reality. Small changes all, unless it is a case of "A little less,/And what a world away!" The shift from God to ultimate reality, or from the Trinity to a "meaningful" explanation of how ultimate reality is encountered by us, may after all be revolutionary, if it involves a quiet substitution of the religion we think we "need" to have our faith meaningful. The New Order may actually be a "world away" from historic Christianity.

To investigate this possibility, though, we might be wise to leave the "instructor" and return to hear what the "head of the department" has to say.

FIVE

CLEARING A SPACE FOR RELIGION

"The necessity for the name 'God' lies in the fact that our being has depths which naturalism . . . cannot or will not recognize."

— *John A. T. Robinson,* Honest To God

If a good part of the appeal of Robinson's *Honest To God* lay in its issuing a manifesto vague enough to permit people to get enthusiastic over its challenge without worrying too much over the details of its program, that did not mean it had no cutting edge at all. It was not merely a rhetorical appeal to march into the future, sight unseen. The shape of a New Theology was visible in it, to be sure, although perhaps the contours were rather blurred. Part of the honesty Robinson felt compelled to live up to was being prepared to point out the direction he felt the Christian faith must take in order to meet the future, even when he was not quite sure about the road, how far it could be travelled, or where exactly it would come out at the end.

An indication of his stance is given in the title of his recent book *But That I Can't Believe.* In choosing this title for a collection of short articles, nearly all of which are about what he *does* believe, the bishop shows his continuing preoccupation with the need of the times (as he sees it) for being presented with a statement of Christian truth in terms that are understandable in these days, and that do not give the impression of being outdated conclusions of ways of thinking long since abandoned by educated men.

This central concern of Robinson's work in the area of

"apologetics," or commending the Christian faith to his contemporaries, was something that came across loud and clear in *Honest To God*. Less clear there were the actual proposals for translating the Christian message to meet the need of the times for new understanding, since confident statements about moving to fresh categories of thought were apt to be followed by qualifications that seemed to restore to tradition territory that had previously been declared abandoned.

Because of Robinson's refusal to follow the logic of the New whenever this threatened to imperil the Old — a refusal that has become increasingly evident in subsequent writings — his significance in the evolution of a New Christianity is often very much underrated. Compared with most of the recent radicals he looks like a dyed-in-the-wool conservative. Yet his importance is not limited to his success in giving an initial impetus to a New Theology by catchng the public attention with his conviction that faith must be cast in a new mold. As I argued in the previous chapter, his strategic place in the history of the "radical" movement certainly makes his contribution of larger significance than the contributions of later, more spectacularly revolutionary radicals. But, in addition, his thinking is particularly valuable in showing the basic issues involved in the movement. Others have followed one line to the limit, seeking in secularity, or the death of God, or the New Morality, or some other "radical" perspective on faith to find *the* form of religion for contemporary man. Robinson has tried to look to the New and also to hold on to the Old. In this attempt, he exposes quite admirably the tensions present in the different approaches to fashion a New Christianity for our age.

In the present chapter I shall explore some of these tensions as displayed in Robinson's thinking.

Honest To God saw in the different contributions of Bultmann, Tillich, and Bonhoeffer a single pointer towards the emerging shape of faith that was to dominate the future. Of the three theologians, Bultmann most obviously shared his concern for bringing the modern statement of Christian belief into line with the world-view of modern man. It had been Bultmann's missionary zeal that had inspired his program for demythologizing the Bible. Believing that the "scandal" of Christian faith lay altogether in the challenge of the gospel to men in every age to decide for or against faith in the saving power of Jesus Christ, Bultmann wished to remove the false "scandal" or obstacle in the way of modern man's being challenged by faith that was located in the language of the Bible. The Bible assumed an ancient world-view of three levels: heaven above, the earth in the middle, and hell below. Today we have an altogether different picture of the universe, gained for us through the discoveries of science. Therefore, if we are to see what the Bible is really talking about when it talks about salvation through Jesus Christ, we must "demythologize" the language of the Bible by dissociating the idea of salvation from a divine Being who came down from heaven, descended into hell, and ascended again into heaven. Only then, freed of its associations with an outmoded world-view, will salvation stand forth in its true meaning as an ever-present experience of God's power to remake us and to renew us in our human existence.

Honest To God gave prominence to the need to rid ourselves of the antique picture of a "three-decker" universe. But it also shied away from following Bultmann's demythologizing program too closely, on the grounds that there were too many of Bultmann's highly debatable personal opinions tied into the program. Robinson used Bonhoeffer's criticism of Bultmann, citing his opinion that Bultmann, in one direction, had not "gone far enough," since modern man may be coming to the stage where he will live entirely without any "God-hypothesis." According to Robinson, Bonhoeffer's radical vision added one more argument in support of the widespread view that the traditional understanding of God as a Being "above" the world had become bankrupt. He then turned to a consideration of what view of God might be acceptable to the man of today, finding that the objections of many nineteenth- and twentieth-century thinkers to a supernatural God ("The Old Man in the Sky") could best be met by Paul Tillich's characterization of God as ultimate reality and the Ground of our being.

It is rather revealing that Robinson, who was willing to quote a criticism of Bultmann from Bonhoeffer's *Letters and Papers from Prison,* did not quote also a criticism of Tillich from the same source. Bonhoeffer wrote that Tillich was prominent among those who had as their objective "the clearing of a space for religion in the world or against the world."

Bonhoeffer's criticism of Tillich would seem to have something to say quite directly to Robinson's eager adoption of Tillich's view of God. Since the idea of a supernatural God "above" the world is no longer acceptable to present-day ways of thinking, then a God "in the depths" must be substituted. The inference was that there was no space for God "up there" now that we could explore the spaces above our planet. But there was room for a God in the depths — especially in the depths of human consciousness — since there was still a need to explain the continued existence of religious experience in the human heart. Man could therefore still keep on being religious, in the way that he had always been, only the new explanation of the religious impulse would be rooted in his own internal experience rather than in the idea that the external world had been created by a deity who existed somehow "out there" in some supernatural realm. Only think of God as ultimate reality, urged Robinson, and then God becomes something no one can deny.

Robinson sought to bring Tillich's understanding of a God in the depths into line with Bonhoeffer's view that Christianity was outgrowing religion by saying that Tillich too did not locate his ultimate reality in any exclusive "religious" sphere but found this reality diffused throughout all experience. But that is only to say (using Bonhoeffer's terms) that Tillich was not one of those who tried to clear a space for religion *against* the world. Finding a space for religion against the world would indeed divide human experience into two parts: the "worldly" ("secular," "profane") over against the "religious" ("churchly," "sacred"). In this view the religious person withdraws in hostility from everything worldly in order to cultivate religion in its purity. Tillich, however, was one who tried to clear a space for religion *in* the world. He saw religion as "the depth dimension" of experience, and so as an aspect of all human consciousness. Culture, he liked to say, is the form of religion, while religion is the substance of culture.

Thus Tillich wished to clear a space for religion that was as wide as the world and that permeated the whole of experience. It was only on the surface of life that the world did not seem to be conscious of the reality of religion. Naturalism saw no

48

space for God in the world because it looked too superficially at human existence. Once a deeper and more searching vision of life was adopted, all things could be seen in a religious perspective. The universal basis for all religion was seeing the holy in the finite, and that vision was open to all men at all times if they only recognized their essential humanity. They could see there was a space for God in the depths of existence. A supernatural God, on the other hand, must be rejected because his "dwelling place" could not be vouched for by human experience.

Bonhoeffer's vision of a "worldly" Christianity need not be described at this point, except that it must be understood as having nothing to do with overcoming naturalism by positing the necessity of recognizing the religious dimension of existence. At the moment I wish simply to bring out the contrast between Bonhoeffer's and Tillich's thinking about religion. For Bonhoeffer man can, and perhaps should, learn to do without religion; for Tillich religion is the perennial concern of mankind, which, when ignored, comes back in impoverished and perverted forms. For Bonhoeffer Christianity is not just one version of religion but the overcoming of religion; for Tillich Christianity cannot be understood without first understanding the nature of religion and afterwards finding how the universal themes of religion are embodied in particular forms by the Christian religion. For Bonhoeffer Jesus Christ is God's unique revelation; for Tillich revelation is given in revelatory experiences, among which is the experience of Jesus as the Christ (that is, as the symbol of the ultimate). Of course, Tillich's view of religion as the depths of man's spiritual life supposes that the attempts to embody religion in specific forms — all religions — are partial and inadequate attempts to realize the wholeness of religion. Yet all have truth insofar as they point us to the depth of our experience and disclose ultimate reality.

Much was involved when Robinson decided to base his reconstructed picture of God principally upon Tillich's presentation of God as ultimate reality, the Ground of man's own being and not a separate Being over against man. To begin with, God as a hypothesis to explain the world was placed firmly in the foreground. Bultmann's objection to the "three-decker" universe as presented in the Bible was given prominence. The implication drawn from this was that the "basic structure" (Robinson's phrase) of traditional thinking about God must be changed. That is to say, the world-view of modern man demands a different kind of God from a supernatural Being. *That* hypothesis no longer is attractive, so another hypothesis must be brought forward. The notion of a God-in-the-depths is a hypothesis that explains man's present idea of "the ultimate significance of the constitution of the universe" (Robinson's phrase again), and on that account is worthy to be entertained. When you plan to clear a space for religion in the world, naturally your picture of the world determines the kind of space you believe you are permitted to clear. Every time you alter your mental picture, you are bound to feel that you need quite a different God to fit the new space.

Then, in the second place, Tillich's God-in-the-depths discovered through revelatory experiences has no necessary connection with the revelation of God in Jesus Christ. Even if the Christian gospel is said to embody *final* revelation, as Tillich liked to say, nevertheless the authority allowing us to affirm this judgment must come out of the depths of our being and not from the gospel itself. The testimony of the Bible and the Church is subject to our estimate of how far this testimony reflects religious reality and how far it stands in need of correction in the light of other revelatory experiences we have access to. Our view of what religion ought to be and to do has the first and last word on the adequacy of Christian faith to fit our religious needs.

Robinson is clearly committed to upholding not only the finality but also the authority of Christian revelation. In the *Honest To God Debate* he contributed an essay "The Debate Continues" in which, replying to criticism of his Tillichian statement that the question of God was the question of whether the depth of being was a reality, he conceded that he was prepared to alter his statement in order to affirm that the God he believed in was the Father, Son, and Spirit of Christian revelation. He wrote in the same essay, "The only question at issue is *how* the biblical doctrine is to be given expression today, in a non-supernaturalistic world-view." Yet, if "biblical doctrine" really was his concern, surely the first answer to give to the question was, "By refusing to state the reality of God in terms

50

which treat the nonsupernaturalistic world-view as though it were an absolute, and so make God a prisoner of this view." He also might have taken some hints from Bonhoeffer on how to escape from absolutizing this world-view by holding on to the biblical understanding of God as the one before whom we stand. But more of that later (see Chapters 7 and 8).

I have given this chapter over to discussing *Honest To God* because its author occupies so intriguing a place in the recent development of the New Theology. Uninterested himself in initiating any New Theology, and indeed specifically disclaiming any part in it, he nevertheless has been more influential than any other single person in giving currency to the idea that we must push on towards a New Christianity adapted to the needs of contemporary man. His desire has been simply to state historic Christian doctrine in terms understandable today. Yet the outcome of his intervention on the theological scene has been to convince many people that historic Christian doctrine was for a past that has come to an end and today is meaningless. The reason for this paradox seems to be (if my analysis has been at all to the point) that his starting-point in Tillich's religious philosophy, and his interpretation of Bonhoeffer as someone whose ideas were compatible with Tillich's, has reinforced the belief that our prime task today is the construction of a God-hypothesis in line with the modern world-view repudiating supernaturalism.

In the next chapter I shall look at some of the God-hypotheses proposed by other thinkers, more "radical" than Robinson, who believe they have particular insights into the outlook of contemporary man, and so can give their individual reports on the space currently available for religion.

SIX

SOME GOD-HYPOTHESES

An honest God's the noblest work of man.
— *Samuel Butler,* Further Extracts
from the Notebooks

The Secular Meaning of the Gospel by Paul van Buren was judged by many on its appearance in 1963 to be a radically new attempt to interpret Christianity for the times. Robinson stated that it seemed to bear out his conviction, expressed in *Honest To God,* that his own book, if it erred, "will be seen to have erred in not being nearly radical enough" (p. 250). At the time, it seemed as though van Buren had gone almost to the limit of theological extremism, for the central proposal in the book was that the time had passed when we could continue to speak about God at all. Henceforth Christian faith must be rooted in what we knew about the human figure of Jesus and his influence upon us.

Bonhoeffer was the outstanding theological influence upon van Buren's thinking, or so it seemed from references through the book (which was prefixed by W. H. Auden's fine poem "Friday's Child"). Van Buren expressed the opinion that his work might show one way of working out Bonhoeffer's hints of "a non-religious interpretation of biblical concepts." The other prominent influence was that of British linguistic philosophy. From this philosophy van Buren took the principles that guided him in deciding that no meaning could be attached by modern man to the word "God." Since our outlook today was empirically based, rejecting all notions of a "reality" not to be found in our concrete experience of this world we live in, both the supernatural God and the notion of a transcendent "ultimate reality" were thrown out. Although Tillich's philosophical theology was not considered directly in van Buren's book, those of Bultmann and his followers in the existentialist camp were discussed very fully; and their appeal to the experience of "transcendence" and "ground and end of all things" was rejected outright as being meaningless to the contemporary man with his feet firmly planted on the soil of this world.

Van Buren's argument is that we know only of one world, namely, the empirical world that science explores and common sense recognizes as a world of things and people. Therefore Jesus, a historical being like ourselves, is the sole approach to Christian faith. This Jesus was a man like other men, yet in one respect he was different from all other men. His life displayed a unique quality, which was a quality of perfect freedom. Free himself, he set others free by a kind of "contagion." Thus the Christian faith is solidly based in the one world we know. It lives and endures because Christians share a common historical perspective that sees in Jesus the source of a gospel that is truly good news for modern, secular men. All that the early Christian creeds meant when they spoke of two natures — divine and human — in the person of Jesus Christ is essentially preserved in this "non-religious interpretation of biblical concepts." The secular believer accepts Jesus of Nazareth as a man who once lived a sinless ("free") life, but who also, as has happened since the first Easter Day, has become the Saviour ("liberator") to whom Christians are committed.

The Secular Meaning of the Gospel is an almost perfect example, not of religionless Christianity, but of its opposite, a religion constructed around a God-hypothesis. The only thing that might conceal this otherwise transparent fact about van Buren's religious construction is that he has placed an embargo on the word "God." His world-view will not permit the use of this word among those who have sworn loyalty to the "secular" perspective. But we all know very well how it is one thing to lay down ideological prescriptions and another to live by them. The declaration that class distinctions have been abolished in Communist society does little to impede the growth of class distinctions in Communist societies. And my protestation that I am immune from superstitions, but have refused to take my place at a dinner-table set for thirteen merely because I happen to feel that way, is likely to be received with polite skepticism. When van Buren says that the word "God" is meaningless to modern man, but that modern man can still respond in faith to Jesus as a liberator — meaning by that what Christians used to mean by speaking of the divinity of Jesus — then clearly his outlook still embraces the "divine."

Van Buren counters the suggestion that his proposal for a secular Christianity reduces faith to ethics, whereas Christianity is much more than that, by asking what, *in secular terms,* that "more" could possibly be. The answer to this rhetorical question is surely that he himself has covertly inserted the "more" under the heading of ethical behavior. He has cleared a space for religion within the secular world-view. This religious space lies within the ethical, but is more than the ethical. And the God who can be made to fit into the space is a power moving in the ethical to give the ethical a more than ordinary significance. Van Buren's God-hypothesis is the presence of the liberating power of the "contagion" spread by Jesus after the first Easter Day.

Now, in connection with any world-view, no God-hypothesis can do other than fit the space cleared for religion there. To change the metaphor, when you cut your coat according to the cloth, if you allow only a very little cloth you will end up with only a very small coat. Van Buren's God is restricted to the sphere of ethics and to the personal perspective upon life that commits an individual to a certain course of ethical action. As a result, this God is not permitted to have his own transcendent existence, to be called by a definite name, or — which amounts to the same thing — to be thought of as personal. But he is still there. He is a unique and all-important power commanding absolute loyalty; and so he is worthy of the title of God, even if van Buren, for reasons of his own, withholds the title. And he is still transcendent, in the way in which ultimate reality transcends everyday reality, or else there is no point in being particularly excited when we find that Jesus of Nazareth makes us free.

Van Buren confesses that it is precisely because *a transcendent element* enters into the experience of choosing the freedom given by Jesus of Nazareth that this experience becomes an experience of faith. Consequently, we feel ourselves to be chosen, not choosing. The recognition of such a transcendent element calling forth the response of faith reveals that van Buren recognizes the divinity of the power he described. The fact that, in deference to the empirical framework within which he has decided to place his religious philosophy, he stops short of calling the power "God" is of little moment. We may think that his decision reflects a prejudice, and confuses the issue; or we may think that van Buren wants to avoid entangling his God-the-power-within-life with traditional conceptions of God-above-the-world. Either way, the important fact is that he has called us to recognize the presence of a transcendent reality which both demands our allegiance and creates in us the willing response of faith. Nothing less than divinity can do that. Van Buren has injected into the empirical world a transcendent element making the ethical more than ethical. To find liberation through the contagious freedom of Jesus of Nazareth is not merely a good thing to find. It is the one thing needful, the passport to the Kingdom of Heaven.

Actually, van Buren's prescription for a secular gospel is remarkably like previous attempts in the nineteenth century to construct a revised Christianity on an ethical foundation. Matthew Arnold, that good Victorian moralist, also fastened on the unique influence of Jesus of Nazareth as the one aspect of the Christian story that made sense to the contemporary man of his day. I can find no essential difference between van Buren's "secular meaning" of the gospel and Arnold's rejection of a supernatural Christ in favor of a new reading of Christianity based on what he called its "natural truth." Arnold, too, pointed to the power that was evident in the person of Jesus to liberate men ethically. Only he did not hesitate to call this power the reality of God at work in Jesus. Instead of refusing to speak of God, he redefined God as "the power not ourselves that makes for righteousness." In this he was more consistent than van Buren, who posits a transcendent element in the secular Christian's experience that elicits faith, and then leaves faith with nothing transcendent to latch on to. Though unwilling to use the word "God," van Buren still has to speak somehow of the power-not-ourselves (it chooses us!) without which the gap between Jesus, the excellent example of a free man, and Jesus, the transformer of our existence, would remain unbridged. Evidently,

55

van Buren's secular left hand does not know what his religious right hand is doing when the latter starts constructing its God-hypothesis.

Whenever Christian faith is reinterpreted in order to make it conform to a particular world-view, a new God-hypothesis has to be proposed. It is logically impossible to suggest any fresh interpretation that lacks an effective substitute for the super-natural God of Christian tradition or which claims to be con-sistently "atheistic." This is the lesson which van Buren's ven-ture into empirical Christianity teaches us. And a similar lesson may be learned from so-called Christian atheism.

Van Buren did not choose to use the term "death of God" in *The Secular Meaning of the Gospel*. Yet, understandably, his belief that the Christian gospel could continue to be proclaimed without using the word "God" connected him in the public mind with those who affirmed that "God is dead." And the link was a real one. If God ceases to be thought of as a Being "above" the world, and is pictured as a power manifest in the world, then the new God-hypothesis can be entertained only when the previous understanding of divinity has been destroyed. The supernatural God must be "killed" in order for the God who is the transcendent element in experience (or the God in the depths) to live. Another way of saying the same thing is that, when you clear a space for religion in the world, you can only allow in that space one God: the God who fits the space, the God-hypothesis tailored to the cloth of one particular world-view.

The metaphor of the "death" of God is a very apt one to apply when the God one has in mind is a God-hypothesis. When one entertains a new God-hypothesis, previous hypotheses be-come dead. William James used to say that choices in religious loyalties are confined to "live options" — dead options being religious beliefs that had ceased to be attractive.

Tillich considered the supernatural God to be a dead option today, explaining that Nietzsche was right to declare that the God who made him into an object was one who must be killed. It was not without cause that William Hamilton and Thomas Altizer dedicated their *Radical Theology and the Death of God* to the memory of Paul Tillich. No one more than Tillich has established the belief that what modern man needs is a God-hypothesis to round out a world-view; and this belief calls for the "death" of the God of historic Christianity who stands above the world and all human world-views. Yet Tillich himself saw no reason to take up the slogan "God is dead." It is partly a matter of temperament and partly the quality of his particular religious world-view that differentiates his outlook from that of the Christian atheists. While he insisted, "I have fought supernaturalism from my early writings on," his warfare was limited to the plane of academic discussion. So secure was he in his conviction that the word "God" was a universal symbol for faith in ultimate reality that he was willing to assume that there must be more truth than error in any serious use of the symbol, even where the supernaturalistic "distortion" of faith was involved. In particular, the statements contained in his sermons were deliberately worded so that people with very different understandings of the being of God and the nature of religious belief would find nothing offensive to their particular level of faith.

Tillich could rest in the equanimity born of an assurance that the way of thought he espoused had a long, continuous tradition behind it. Linked firmly with the nineteenth century through his own teachers, and looking back along a religious, philosophical, and cultural line stretching from the existentialists to the Greeks, he felt no inclination to set the New in opposition to the Old. The Christian atheists, on the other hand, have obviously been moved by quite different feelings. With them the sense of opposition between the New and the Old plays a very prominent part.

Thomas Altizer, for example, has built his religious philosophy very nearly on the principle that the New must continually be meeting the Old and destroying it. His recent volume *Toward a New Christianity* (1967) is a collection of writings meant to show the "tradition" of Christian atheism. It begins with William Blake and is devoted to nineteenth- and twentieth-century thinkers who, in Altizer's estimation, have challenged the accepted understanding of Christian faith. As Altizer presents his tradition, therefore, it seems to be a very much briefer one than Tillich's, and a continuously revolutionary one. What is important is that revolution is a key concept in Altizer's thinking. He ends the Introduction to his volume by insisting that unless Protestantism today is willing to undergo a "radical transformation" to justify its existence it inevitably will cease to exist.

But then in Altizer's world-view, everything in the universe must always be undergoing radical transformation or it ceases to exist. God himself is a process who goes through successive stages, with each new one cancelling the one before. At any rate, Altizer is no atheist or pseudo-atheist denying that we can continue to use the word "God." His God-hypothesis is tailored to his world-view, which he has built up largely from Hegel and other nineteenth-century thinkers. Because Altizer thinks all life is a process, we only stay alive by turning decisively away from the Old towards the New; otherwise we will be trying fruitlessly to live in a stage in the ongoing process that has already fallen behind us. At present, it seems, we have reached the stage where God is appearing entirely within humanity. If we are to keep in touch with the present form of God, therefore, we must gladly accept the "death" of the former view of a supernatural God above the world in order to be where God himself is.

So in Altizer's writings the understanding of God as a power moving in the world — the idea that was an unacknowledged supposition for van Buren — comes into the center of the picture. Being in touch with the present life of God gives liberating power; losing touch with it through backward-looking spells death. This is a dynamic form of Tillich's God as ultimate reality, who is known in our lives as "the power of being." If we accept the world-view, we must accept the God-hypothesis that fits it. The space that Altizer has cleared for religion in the world can be likened to a moving streetcar that leaves us behind if we do not jump on it. Altizer does not tell us the destination of the streetcar, though, or what happens when we get there.

While Altizer's "Christian atheism" is only atheism in the sense of rejecting a supernatural God in favor of the God-hypothesis that explains the world as process, William Hamilton has all of van Buren's reticence in bringing forward the God-hypothesis he favors, though for a different reason. He does not think modern man, in order to be really modern and secular, cannot use the empirically meaningless word "God." Rather, from reflection upon his own spiritual pilgrimage, he concludes that modern man is discovering that what the word "God" used to mean, though as a word still understandable enough, no longer strikes an answering chord in his present experience. From some of Hamilton's explanations of why he speaks of the death of God it would seem that the situation is rather like that of having an old friend move out of the area, promise to write, but never do so. After a long period of silence one must presume the friend dead; at any rate, the friendship is dead and one had better find new friends.

If Altizer likes to survey world history as a process of continual change through revolutionary upheavals, Hamilton pays little attention to comprehensive theories about the universe and concentrates upon the changing moods and fashions of recent years. He enjoys commenting on the passing show of culture, and trying to catch and identify current trends and "styles." His thinking is impressionistic, fluid, and apt to take sudden turns and change gears unexpectedly. Because he outlines no overall world-view, his version of Christian atheism seems to propose no definite God-hypothesis.

Nevertheless, the God-hypothesis is there all right, though concealed under cover of apparently tentative and provisional estimates of "a place to stand" today. Insofar as Hamilton is prepared to stand upon some convictions and to make a few definite proposals concerning the "style" of faith suitable for the 1960s, we can see the shape of the space he wants to clear for religion. (A recent article of his was called "The Shape of a Radical Theology.") He emphasizes such themes as the experience of the permanent absence of God, obedience to Jesus the ethical teacher, involvement in the world's problems, a spirit of optimism, and a will to love that is not weakened but actually strengthened by the absence of faith. And he insists that he believes there is a "theology" in all this, not just a humanism with a Christian flavor. Well, if his position is more than a purely individual one but is set out as a model suitable for adoption by contemporary Christians, he is certainly not offering us a theology, a "science of divinity," minus anything divine. His God-hypothesis, like van Buren's, must try to account for the "more" that is in the human Jesus, that which makes him more than another good example of how to live as a human being. It must explain why there is "a place to stand" in love and optimistic engagement in the betterment of life for our brothers, and why the absence of a supernatural God helps rather than hinders our life as Christians.

Hamilton's eagerness to record the latest change in the social mood, and his evident (though unspoken) conviction that the place to stand is where he can have his hand on the pulse of contemporary man so as not to miss any variation in the heart-beat of culture — these things point to his belief that there is a revelation for us in those aspects of the world about us that reflect human self-consciousness. His God is the one who speaks in society's cultural achievements, and whose voice is heard by the sensitive reader of the poets and commentators upon man's discovery of his powers to enlarge and dignify his life. Man today, therefore, should be eager to say a final farewell to the God "above" the world in order to be free to give his undivided loyalty to the God in the depths of his own spirit, who lives in the human world of man's creation.

The God-hypothesis bound up with William Hamilton's world-view appears in a much more direct form in the writings of Werner and Lotte Pelz, who speak, from the other side of the Atlantic, for the outlook of Christian atheism which has been better known in its American versions. The title page of the Pelzes' *God Is No More* carries the quotation from William Blake (one of Altizer's favorite sources):

> *If Thou humblest Thyself, Thou humblest Me.*
> *Thou also dwell'st in Eternity.*
> *Thou art a Man: God is no more:*
> *Thy own Humanity learn to adore,*
> *For that is My spirit of life.*

The supernatural God is no more, for divinity is no more than man's transcendent imagination.

The Pelzes' appeal is to the words of Jesus, interpreted as communications from one man conscious of the potentialities latent in humanity to all who find his words true for themselves. They believe that the real mistake of the early Church was to try to make Jesus into a God — and therefore to dehumanize him, to make him into something other than man. The understanding they have of our capacity to take Jesus as our guide to all human truth is that we, like him, know eternity in our own experience. The human imagination has the capacity to manu-

60

facture gods, and then to allow itself to be bound by its own creations. But today we need no longer turn back in slavery to empty ideas, the products of our own fears and refusal to live creatively. Jesus calls us to abundant, imaginative life. God is no more, because we have outgrown the need for all projections of the prohibitive conscience. And Jesus is our guarantee that the new way of freedom to live without God is possible. The Resurrection — no mere event but an eternal fact — is our call to take this life and this earth seriously.

The Pelzes insist that they have no system, and that all systems are misleading. There may be a good deal of truth in their second statement, but they can hardly stand behind their first one and also quote William Blake on the identity of God and Man. Blake insisted, "I must create my own system or else be enslaved by another man's." The Pelzes' appeal to the words of Jesus, authenticated authoritatively by their own consciousness, cannot be upheld except by an explicit or implicit assumption of a universe in which human consciousness is essentially eternal and divine. Their "system" excludes a supernatural God, and makes revelation a "recognition" of man's intrinsic divinity. Here the space cleared for religion is the sphere of the human imagination, and the God who rules over this sphere is the power of humanity as such to direct its own destiny by creating its own eternity in time. God must be no more, since if he were still around his existence would cause the collapse of the Pelzes' system and evaporate the plausibility of their interpretation of Jesus.

In the title essay of his *The Reality of God and Other Essays* Schubert M. Ogden discusses the way in which "religion in its various forms" uses the word "God." He writes, "I hold that the primary use or function of 'God' is to refer to the objective ground in reality itself of our ineradicable confidence in the final worth of our existence" (p. 37). It seems to me that Ogden's statement describes quite accurately how all varieties of religion, diverse as they may be, actually proceed to offer us a God and ask us to believe in him. Because different religions have different ideas about what gives worth to our existence (and about what our existence "really" is), so they suggest a wide range of

"Gods" for our approval. Where there is no agreement about world-views, we need not expect agreeing God-hypotheses, and far less a single God-hypothesis. Each will tell us that our "real" need is to find a certain support in order to have continued trust in the worth of our existence, and offer us a God who will look after us in this respect.

In this chapter I have looked at a few of the "Gods" offered by different varieties of "Christian atheists." All of them are surprisingly reticent about the fact that they are offering us a special type of God or any God at all. This may be the result of their eagerness to convince us that they are actually showing us the true, relevant, and contemporary type of Christianity rather than another religion entirely. Perhaps they realize that so-called post-Christian man is still unwilling to think that there can be any genuine religion other than Christianity.

Yet they all, in point of fact, "refer to the objective ground" for our confidence that life is worth living. They point to the reality of contagious freedom, of ever-changing life-process, of the resilience of human love, or of the imaginative experience of eternity in time, and tell us that faith in these will give us abundant life. They unite in looking for the evidence of these worth-supporting realities in the quality of the human life of Jesus. And they ask us to ignore the fact that the Bible and the Church, the witnesses to the Christian gospel through the centuries, have taught that Jesus is Lord for Christians because he is the revelation of the Father, God Almighty, Maker of heaven and earth. Their explanation is that Jesus simply used the language of his time in referring to such a God, but he *really* referred to another reality, a reality modern men with their modern world-view can still believe in after they have ceased to believe in any supernatural Being. This being the case, it is strange that they refer so indirectly, and sketch in so lightly, the features of the "God" whom they suppose to be revealed through Jesus. Are they afraid that, if they spoke out, we might reject their God-hypothesis?

The question remains, however, as to whether there is any genuine alternative to having a world-view and then proposing a God to fit it. Since we certainly do not picture the universe in the same way as Christians of the first, or the sixth, or the sixteenth century pictured it, can we still believe in the same

God? Dietrich Bonhoeffer, who believed that God need not be a hypothesis — and, if he was, was not the God revealed in Jesus Christ — may help us to answer this question.

Part 3

ABOUT BONHOEFFER'S "WORLDLY" CHRISTIANITY

SEVEN

THE GOD WHO IS NOT A HYPOTHESIS

In my sleep He watches yearning
and restores my soul
so that each recurring morning
love and goodness make me whole.
Were God not there,
his face not near,
He had not led me out of fear.
All things have their time and sphere:
God's love lasts forever.

— Paul Gerhardt
(quoted by Dietrich Bonhoeffer,
Letters and Papers from Prison, *p. 90)*

Few passages in any book have caused more ink to be pressed out of typewriter ribbons during the past few years than the pages in Dietrich Bonhoeffer's *Letters and Papers from Prison* where he laid out some brief and tentative sketches for "a non-religious interpretation of biblical terminology."

Some commentators have imagined that these pages prove Bonhoeffer to be breaking with his previous views and launching out into entirely new territory which only now, in the secular sixties, we are able to appreciate and explore on his behalf. Was this the charter for a New Christianity? Granted that the statements he made in these crucial pages are open to different interpretations (and what written words are not?), I should personally answer this question with an unhesitating No. Certainly, Bonhoeffer glimpsed new vistas opening for the communication of the Christian gospel, and did not live to walk

67

down them. But what he saw and recorded, though tantalizingly incomplete, is not in the main open to doubt; and it is so much of a piece with the vision of Christian truth that had inspired his previous writings that its character is unmistakable. The theme he so often stated was being developed in a particular direction. And this theme was that Christianity is not just one more of man's religions, and that the God and Father of our Lord Jesus Christ is not just one more hypothesis to round out a world-view.

The argument in *Letters and Papers from Prison* about the desirability of developing a nonreligious interpretation of biblical concepts stems from Bonhoeffer's reading of the movement of Western culture over the past three hundred years or so. He speaks of *"one* great development which leads to the idea of the autonomy of the world" (p. 217). This is the development seen in all cultural fields, in philosophy, politics, law, science, and morals, whereby the focus of interest has been turned from the divine to the human, from ultimate questions to practical questions, and from life seen in the perspective of eternity to life seen as something valuable in itself. Among the examples Bonhoeffer gives of this historical development is the attempt made by the great seventeenth-century jurist Grotius to develop a basis for international law that would be still accepted as valid for all human society *etsi deus non daretur* — even if God were not in the picture. Another example plays a part in his "Outline for a Book" on the subject of nonreligious Christianity. Here he remarks that the growth of insurance is a phenomenon of Western culture, marking a stage in Western man's achievement of autonomy. Whereas in earlier periods man had to struggle against nature and looked to divine assistance when he needed help, now the possibility of insuring oneself against disasters indicated the measure of the extent to which man has been able to control his environment and bend nature to his will. The upshot of all this is that God is no longer needed to explain the world or to help man to get along comfortably in it. As a working hypothesis he is expendable.

In such a situation, Bonhoeffer continues, nervous souls begin to ask what room there is for God now. Some of them see no hope except to return to the earlier "ages of faith" when God was felt to be needed, and so was worshipped. But he himself believes there is no honest or responsible way of trying merely to put back the clock. He writes,

> And the only way to be honest is to recognize that we have to live in the world *etsi deus non daretur*. And this is just what we do see — before God! So our coming of age forces us to a true recognition of our situation *vis à vis* God. God is teaching us that we must live as men who can get along very well without him. The God who is with us is the God who forsakes us (Mark 15:34). The God who makes us live in this world without using him as a working hypothesis is the God before whom we are ever standing. Before God and with him we live without God (p. 219).

The interesting thing about this passage is how Bonhoeffer finds no problem in saying that God has gone as a working hypothesis and yet is present to us as fully as ever. We do not need religion, and yet we need to quote the New Testament. Our "coming of age" is a lesson God has forced on us to give us the opportunity to know him better by not "using" him. In other words, Bonhoeffer believes that, while the coming of the "religionless" world-view is a fortunate development, we are not bound to it. Our faith is not limited by either its affirmations or its negations. And the God whom we trust does not have to conform to its dictates or be fashioned according to its prescriptions.

It is right here, where God's freedom from our world-view is asserted, that we can see how many who claim to have learned from Bonhoeffer what a religionless Christianity must be have not listened to the first thing he says. While some timid souls imagine that the world-view asking us to live *etsi deus non daretur,* if allowed to continue, must inevitably destroy faith, other equally timid souls take heart at Bonhoeffer's words about not being afraid to come of age. The latter then go hat in hand to the godless world-view and ask to be allowed to continue to call themselves Christians, on the understanding that they will believe nothing that is contrary to the presuppositions of the world-view. Emboldened by the assurance that they are now on the side of progress and enlightenment, they next turn round and inform all other Christians that the submission to the godless world-view is really the only course open to modern Christians, and that adopting the perspective of this world-view will open their eyes for the first time to the true meaning of Christian faith.

I do not think that this is at all a caricature of what has been done under the guise of accepting, with Bonhoeffer, man's coming of age. Theologians actually have asked the question which Bonhoeffer thought to be a faithless question, namely, "What room is there left for God now?" And they have been willing to accept as an answer to their question, "Since God is no longer in the picture you must make do with the divinity residing in humanity. Apparently, you would like to call yourselves Christians still. Well, Jesus was a man *and* divine, according to your traditional Christian formula. If you pick some aspect of his humanity and say your faith is in *that*, no one will object much to a God resident in a human quality, especially if you are careful also to point out that your peculiar beliefs do not prevent you from devoting yourselves heart and soul to what everyone today knows is the real end of life: building a community giving full scope to human creativity."

As human beings, of course, Christians will never wish to dissociate themselves from the creative human goals that their generation is striving to reach. That is why Bonhoeffer is so sure we cannot put the clock back or seek to return to an earlier cultural environment. Yet at no time in his career was Bonhoeffer willing to agree that the Christian's goals were identical with the goals of contemporary culture or the content of revelation reducible to natural human aspirations. The "worldly" Christianity he hoped to see taking the place of "ecclesiastical interests" was not just a baptized worldliness, a humanism given a religious blessing. A holy worldliness — yes; but that is something else, for it assumes the concern of a Paul to be all things to all men in the interests of a Kingdom that cannot be a kingdom of this world.

The quotation from *Letters and Papers from Prison* given above, which follows Bonhoeffer's musings about the impossibility of our returning to our cultural childhood, is preceded by the sentence, "The only way is that of Matthew 18:3, i.e. through repentance, through *ultimate* honesty." It is extremely unfortunate that Christians who have echoed his words about honesty as the foremost demand of our day have mostly stopped short with the thought that we have to show our honesty by not ignoring the claims of contemporary thought, and have failed to notice Bonhoeffer's insistence upon ultimate honesty with regard to New Testament claims. The repentance of Matthew 18:3 is, preeminently, repentance of our worldly wisdom that imagines the current world-view to be the judge of all things in heaven and earth. Those who have been given the grace to become little children know that nothing can be so obtusely, ignorantly, wickedly self-deceiving as the so-called adult mind. Nothing else is so ready to usurp the place of God and to be dogmatic about what can and what cannot be believed.

Now, there are a good many sayings of Bonhoeffer that seem to suggest that he expected a "worldly" Christianity to concentrate upon the human Jesus because this was the one point of contact with an age that had thrown overboard the notion of the supernatural and recognized nothing except the empirical order of nature and wholly human experience. There is some justification for reading Bonhoeffer along this line; but it is far from being the whole truth. Consider, for example, his statement about God and transcendence in the "Outline for a Book." He says, under the heading of Chapter 2, which was to be called "The Real Meaning of the Christian Faith":

> What do we mean by 'God'? Not in the first place an abstract belief in his omnipotence, etc. That is not a genuine experience of God, but a partial extension of the world. Encounter with Jesus Christ, implying a complete orientation of human being in the experience of Jesus as one whose only concern is for others. This concern of Jesus for others the experience of transcendence. This freedom from self, maintained to the point of death, the sole ground of his omnipotence, omniscience and ubiquity. Faith is participation in this Being of Jesus (incarnation, cross and resurrection). Our relation to God not a religious relationship to a supreme Being, absolute in power and goodness, which is a spurious conception of transcendence, but a new life for others, through participation in the Being of God. The transcendence consists not in tasks beyond our scope and power, but in the nearest thing [neighbor] to hand. God in human form, not, as in other religions, in animal form — the monstrous, chaotic, re-mote and terrifying — nor yet in abstract form — the absolute, metaphysical, infinite, etc. — nor yet in the Greek divine-human of autonomous man, but man existing for others, and hence the Crucified. A life based on the transcendent (pp. 237f.).

71

I have quoted the whole paragraph because isolated sentences and, still more, phrases can so easily give the wrong impression. "Encounter with Jesus Christ, implying a complete orientation of human being in the experience of Jesus as one whose only concern is for others." That sentence might be read as an invitation to find divinity purely in the humanity of Jesus, whose acts illustrate the essential human quality of compassion and so serve to illuminate the truth that "human being" is the sole place where divinity appears in the world. Yet the context makes it clear that Bonhoeffer is ruling out all *generalized* understanding of God. If God is not to be found in the presence of the uncanny, nor in the idea of abstract omnipotence, he is equally not to be found in contemplating in Jesus the appearance of a pure humanity. So to think would be to opt for a version of "the Greek divine-human of autonomous man"— such a version, for example, as Werner and Lotte Pelz adopt when they place their commentary on the words of Jesus under the rubric of William Blake's, "Thou art a Man: God is no more:/Thy own Humanity learn to adore...."

Of course, for Bonhoeffer the Being of Jesus is the incarnation of true humanity, and faith consists in participation in this Being, a life based on genuine transcendence. But, once the transition is made to believing that transcendence is simply a dimension of human experience as such, so that faith is whole-hearted participation in a secular society that has shrugged off outmoded views of a supernatural God, we are back in abstractions. This is simply a religious relationship to a supreme being turned inside out and reappearing as a quasi-religious relationship to the spirit of a secular age. God in human form is God incarnate in the Crucified: in *this man Jesus,* and not in the human sphere as opposed to an "unbelievable" supernatural sphere. Encounter with the Man for Others is not identical with, even if it embraces, the will to be concerned for the well-being of others.

I shall return to this aspect of Bonhoeffer's thought when considering the "secular" in the New Theology. Meanwhile, how does Bonhoeffer expect us to understand his reference to the life of Jesus (and our own lives, insofar as we participate in his) as a life based on the transcendent? The necessary context for this reference is supplied at the conclusion of the passage (quoted earlier in this chapter) about our living without God yet before him. God, he says, allows himself to be edged out of the world and on to the cross. . . . God is weak and powerless in the world. . . .

> This is the decisive difference between Christianity and all religions. Man's religiosity makes him look in his distress to the power of God in the world; he uses God as a *Deus ex machina*. The Bible however directs him to the powerlessness and the suffering of God; only a suffering God can help. To this extent we may say that the process we have described by which the world came of age was an abandonment of a false conception of God, and a clearing of the decks for the God of the Bible, who conquers power and space in the world by his weakness. This must be the starting point for our 'worldly' interpretation (p. 220).

Once again, we see that Bonhoeffer's contrast is always between Christian faith and man's religions. While the religious man makes for himself promise to meet his needs with a supply of power, the biblical story points to the Crucified, who is a figure of weakness. Certainly, Christian faith finds in the powerlessness of Jesus Christ upon the cross a force strong enough to conquer "power and space in the world." The cross does not stand alone, since it is found in the setting of the incarnation and the resurrection. Yet, all the time, the powerlessness of the Christian Saviour is all that is actually visible to "the world." That is why the New Testament refers to the preaching of the cross as a stumbling-block and foolishness to cultural man, the man-in-the-street (1 Cor. 1:21-24). And that is why Bonhoeffer welcomed the disappearance of the God-hypothesis from twentieth-century man's thinking about the world. It seemed to him that it was a great gain not to have people expecting Christianity to give them the kind of uplift they expected religion to provide. One of the developments of modern life that gave him no pleasure at all was the popularity of psychiatry, and the prevalence of the notion that Christianity had much the same aim and purpose as psychiatric treatment, namely, to help us achieve inner strength and the peace of mind that goes with an integrated personality. Such an outlook, he considered, was sending us straight back to the old mistake of trying to make a need-satisfying religion out of Christian faith.

In Christ as the Man for Others, so Bonhoeffer believed,

was the way of our deliverance from a religion satisfying our needs. Yet we should not overlook how easily the motif of serving others, if generalized and made into a simple possibility for action, can be turned into a prescription for a religion satisfying our needs — in this case, our need to feel that we are justified by our good works. Yes, transcendence for Bonhoeffer was near at hand, as near as our neighbor. Transcendence, however, was not exhausted by the neighborly relationship, and it assuredly was not to be identified with the human capacity for altruistic love. As ultimate honesty was to be found in repentance, so ultimate love was found in trust in the God who might withhold from us even the strength needed for serving others. One of Bonhoeffer's poetic meditations recorded in *Letters and Papers from Prison,* is headed "Suffering":

> O wondrous change! Those hands, once so strong and active, have now been bound. Helpless and forlorn, you see the end of your deed. Yet with a sigh of relief, you resign your cause to a stronger hand, and are content to do so. For one brief moment you enjoyed the bliss of freedom, only to give it back to God, that he might perfect it in glory (p. 228).

Bonhoeffer's "worldly" Christianity, indeed, like the New Testament to which he sought to be faithful, sees always a double meaning in the word "world." On the one hand, the world is the sphere of God's creative action and the object of his love. God loved the world and sent his Son into the world to save it (John 3:16, 17). On the other hand, the world does not know God, and rejects the Son who is sent (John 1:10, 11; 3:19; 1 Cor. 1:21; 1 John 3:1). So he argued that the world should not be "prematurely written off," as it is in many religions which offer a salvation *out of* the world. Rather, Christian worldliness is learning "to take the world in one's stride," accepting the fact that here is where one has to live. But that is a very different thing from adopting the world's outlook and the world's valuations. The Church, said Bonhoeffer, has become preoccupied with maintaining itself as an institution *in* the world, until it has forgotten that its charge is to speak the word of reconciliation *to* the world.

There is one very revealing passage in *Letters and Papers from Prison* where Bonhoeffer returns to his often repeated theme that Christian faith does not exist in order to give answers to men's problems, so it is just not true to say that Christianity alone has the answers:

> In fact the Christian answers are no more conclusive or compelling than any of the others. Once more, God cannot be used as a stop-gap. We must not wait until we are at the end of our tether: he must be found at the centre of life: in life, and not only in death; in health and vigour, and not only in suffering; in activity, and not only in sin. The ground for this lies in the revelation of God in Christ. Christ is the centre of life, and in no sense did he come to answer our unsolved problems. From the centre of life certain questions are seen to be wholly irrelevant, and so are the answers commonly given to them — I am thinking for example of the judgement pronounced on the friends of Job. In Christ there are no Christian problems (p. 191).

In Christ there are no Christian problems. This is a judgment pronounced against, among other things, the frequently repeated assertion that the chief problem for theology today is the problem of God. For Bonhoeffer, the revelation of God in Christ clears such abstract problems out of the way, so that we can see God in Christ in the center of life: the "beyond" in the midst of life.

Our task as modern men, then, cannot be to take the contemporary world-view so seriously that all we can think of is what concept of God this world-view allows us to have. Instead, our task is to take the revelation of God in Christ, as the New Testament proclaims it, and without trying to "update" it, into the middle of the world we live in. Bonhoeffer wrote:

> The world's coming of age is then no longer an occasion for polemics and apologetics, but it is really better understood than it understands itself, namely on the basis of the Gospel, and in the light of Christ (p. 200).

Bonhoeffer's words recall the reply of Jesus to Peter's confession at Caesarea Philippi, "You did not learn that from mortal man; it was revealed to you by my heavenly Father" (Matt. 16:17). According to Bonhoeffer, Bultmann's demythologizing program was misconceived, because one cannot separate God and miracles. There is no way of accommodating the Christian gospel to the horizons of a world-view that has decided there is no space for the supernatural. The Christian's duty is, first and last, loyalty to the miracle of revelation; and if need be, as he once said, "to wait loyally a whole life time."

Bonhoeffer confessed his ignorance of how the gospel was to be proclaimed "with power" to renew the modern world. Meanwhile, he said, we are being "driven back to first principles" (p. 187), although we hardly know how to speak of the great theological doctrines preserved in the Church — "atonement and redemption, regeneration, the Holy Ghost, the love of our enemies, the cross and resurrection, life in Christ and Christian discipleship." But Christian witness is essential, and will be profitable even in uncertain days. Some of the most moving pages in *Letters and Papers from Prison* are those bearing the heading, "Thoughts on the Baptism of D.W.R." Here Bonhoeffer, deprived of the right to be at the baptism of his baby godson, named after him, addressed the man the baby was to be "if God will and we live." His hope is that his godson will live through the time when Christian witness is "a silent and hidden affair" and see the day when Christians will once again speak openly to all. In any event, he wishes for him that he may prove, through his fidelity to the faith, the scriptural promise that "the path of the righteous is as a shining light, that shineth more and more unto the perfect day (Prov. 4:18)" (p. 188).

During his last days Bonhoeffer wrestled with the problem of how to communicate the gospel. But he never thought the nature of the gospel to be in doubt, or the power of God's grace to be differently manifested now than in former times. How to be a Christian was not a problem to keep us guessing, but a light burden willingly to be taken up and a joy to be explored in trustful assurance.

EIGHT

FAITH AND ITS RELIGIOUS GARMENT

*Religion is the unavoidable reflection in the soul —
in experience — of the miracle of faith which has
occurred to the soul.*

— Karl Barth,
The Epistle to the Romans (6th edition)

In the previous chapter I have tried to bring to the fore how strongly is stressed in Bonhoeffer's *Letters and Papers from Prison* the theme of the independence of the God of Christian revelation from our way of looking at the world. One further quotation may serve to sum up this theme. Bonhoeffer wrote, "The God of Jesus Christ has nothing to do with all that we, in our human way, think he can and ought to do.... One thing is certain: we must always live close to the presence of God, for that is newness of life; and then nothing is impossible, for all things are possible with God" (p. 243).

But, if there were "no problems" in Christ for the Christian, and no doubt concerning "the firm ground on which we stand," problems entered in when it came to a matter of communicating the gospel to men of a particular age. That is why Bonhoeffer gave so much thought to his intuition that there must be a way to give a nonreligious interpretation of biblical concepts, though he never gave any concrete illustrations of how this was to be achieved.

One thing is certain, though. And this is that he never considered, even for a moment, either curtailing the gospel in the interests of making it more palatable to the spirit of the age or watering down its message to make it less offensive,

77

because less "supernatural," to a generation that found no need for the God-hypothesis. When he wished to appeal to any aspect of the Christian revelation, he went straight to either the Old or the New Testament, never hesitating even to quote single texts in order to make a point. His quarrel with Bultmann over demythologizing the New Testament was that Bultmann's program resulted in "abridging the gospel." He added, ". . . whereas I try to think theologically" (p. 167).

For Bonhoeffer to think theologically was to refer to "the great concepts of Christian theology," and he never could have adopted the generalized and worn-down use of the word "theology" — so common at the present moment — to signify merely study in the religious field. So when he said that Bultmann "did not go far enough," he was hardly suggesting that he could have wished Bultmann to have gone on to demythologize the New Testament more thoroughly (since he evidently conceived the basic principle of demythologizing to be mistaken), but rather that he could have wished him to penetrate deeper into his very proper wish to make the New Testament speak directly to modern man. In that case, through adopting the perspective of an adequate theology, he would have seen that what was being demanded was no superficial updating of concepts that had the effect of cutting down the fulness of the gospel message. Rather, it was a much more fundamental reinterpretation that was required, namely, one clearing the decks for the God of the Bible by disentangling biblical concepts from "religion."

Bonhoeffer undoubtedly placed great hopes upon this process of reinterpretation, which is all the more surprising since he himself found it impossible to pass beyond the thought to even one example of a reinterpreted biblical concept. Try as he might, the actual task eluded him. Yet he looked forward with expectation to the day ahead when a new language for communicating the gospel would come with power — "the language of a new righteousness." He believed that he and others were "groping after something new and revolutionary."

Since Bonhoeffer was extremely skeptical about all "apologetic" devices to commend the gospel to mankind, he did not envisage the coming revolution as a matter of language only. The vision he entertained of the words of Christian faith

speaking with strange and startling effect was closely connected
with the renewal he desired for the Church that was to be.
Writing his "Thoughts on the Baptism of D.W.R.," and address-
ing himself to the child who was already, in his imagination,
a type of the Christian of the future, he prophesied that the
old safety and stability that his generation had found in the
ecclesiastical forms of its childhood days would have passed
away for good. The new generation of Christians would grow
up, among open rather than hidden enemies, in a Church that
had been stripped of most of its traditional privileges and had
voluntarily surrendered the rest. This situation would familiar-
ize the Christian with the truth that the life of faith was a
life of warfare, where pain was an ever-present reality and
bearable only because of the assured knowledge of being supported by a community of friends whose loyalty was never
in doubt. In such circumstances, theological thought would
be confined to "responsibility in action," backed by prayer.
Patient waiting would be required until out of this time of
silence came, in due season, the ability to speak freely once
again. Bonhoeffer wrote, "Christian thinking, speaking and
organization must be reborn out of this praying and this
action" (p. 188).

It is the lack of this "existential" setting of the fighting
Christian over against a hostile world that makes it hard to
think that the present moment is the one which Bonhoeffer was
looking forward to so eagerly. Just now many of his admirers
are saying that at last, after a lapse of more than twenty
years, the new day he saw afar off is dawning; and that, by
devoting ourselves with urgent seriousness to the work that
he passed on to us, we can keep faith with his vision. It
would be easier to believe the voices that are saying "lo here!"
and "lo there!" in connection with the promised return of
authentic Christian language if those voices were only a little
less Babel-like and a little more concentrated upon the specifically Christian witness that "worldly" Christianity is now
to make. The new "power" that Bonhoeffer prophesied can
hardly be found in the assurance that the Christian witness is
simply and solely the service of our fellows, together with the
acceptance of a world without God. This solution merely suc-

ceeds in absolutizing the period Bonhoeffer imagined to be an interim.

It is true that William Hamilton, for one, has retained Bonhoeffer's motif of waiting, since he combines with insistence that radical theologians are those who live without God and do not anticipate his return some references to waiting for the possible return of God and a description of the radical Protestant as an individual "caught between a having and a not-having." At least Hamilton leaves the door open to the possibility of our having more in the future than we now have. Meanwhile, however, he insists that the present "experience of the absence of God" is a "theological experience" warranting a theology of the death of God. And, to this extent, he has no intention of waiting before undertaking (and inviting others to undertake) radical Christian thinking and speaking for today. Other spokesmen for "worldly" Christianity, as we have already seen, make no such reservations. They are willing to go right ahead to reduce Christian theology to the limits of a this-worldly perspective, and to call this the theological style for the future.

We may ask, of course, why it was that Bonhoeffer, in the first place, was so certain that Christian thinking, speaking and organization were to find a triumphant rebirth after a time of enforced silence and waiting. If the Christian message is one that presents the powerlessness of God in the midst of worldly powers, we cannot conclude immediately that the language it speaks must necessarily be a language of power. Could not the role of Christian witness be one that does not seek to speak at any time with the confident clarity that the world assumes to be able to command for its own utterances about its own identity and capacities? After all, the Christian knows himself to be a pilgrim upon earth, having no continuing city here in the sphere where the "natural" man feels himself to be so very much at home. If God conquers the power and space of the world by his weakness, Christians may well be most effective when they do not impress the world by the range of their thinking, the forcefulness of their words, or the ingenuity of their organization.

Presumably, what Bonhoeffer looked forward to so eagerly was a Church that should challenge the world directly. One of his favorite themes was the meanness of trying to persuade people to think about God by way of their "inward" private life, where it was thought that they were still vulnerable to being aroused to a sense of guilt. This, he believed, was meeting the world at its point of weakness rather than in its strength — an approach far too "unaristocratic" to be worthy of being allied with the Word of God. The gospel today must address the whole man in the whole of life if it is to be faithful to the biblical message.

But was Bonhoeffer's proposed nonreligious reinterpretation altogether realistic? The fact that he himself could not make the least headway in the matter throws some doubt upon the whole project. Even allowing for the extreme limitations imposed by his condition of imprisonment, one would have imagined that some inkling of the type of reinterpretation required — some specific word of the new language — would have emerged. Yet, for example, the outline of his proposed book keeps entirely to generalized comments on the need for the Church to serve the world and bring its theology to bear on the life of men. On the issue of language it is silent, simply reiterating that such terms as *God* or *transcendence* are not to be interpreted "religiously" or "abstractly."

Previously (in Chapter 3) I have remarked how Bonhoeffer never allowed for the possibility of a return to "religion" such as we have experienced since the end of World War II. He would assuredly have been amazed could he have known how his own example would be quoted to justify fresh attempts to clear a space for religion in the world. We are bound to conclude, nevertheless, that the totally different outcome of the course of history from the one he predicted points to a weakness in his original diagnosis of contemporary culture. I believe that here he very much underestimated the "religious" element in the "world come of age."

Take, for instance, his reference to the way in which Tillich's attempt "to interpret the evolution of the world itself — against its will — in a religious sense" had failed. For him this failure, whereby the world "unseated" Tillich and "went on by itself," was proved by the downfall of the religious socialism, which Tillich supported, when Hitler seized power. So he could not possibly have imagined that Tillich's religious interpretation of the world was to gain so massive a popularity in America during the 1950s that his voice was to be heard again in Europe also and listened to with much greater attention than before 1933. He could not have conceived in his wildest dreams that an Anglican bishop would one day point to Tillich's religious reinterpretation of the word "God" as *the* reinterpretation required for a secular age, coupling Bonhoeffer's own thinking with that of Tillich. At the same time, when he spoke of the (German) world going on by itself, he must have known that it went on, not to a pure secularism, but to a quasi-religious cult of blood and soil having a good deal in common with primitive Germanic paganism.

Again and again, Bonhoeffer seems to turn away from acknowledging the presence of the influence of religion just at the point where it seems he is pointing right to it. Thus, when he names the thinkers who stand out in his mind as being the chief architects of the modern world, he calls them either deists (Descartes, Lord Herbert of Chedbury, Kant) or pantheists (Spinoza, Fichte, Hegel). Strange as we may find the oversight, though, he never stops to ask how far the religious presuppositions of those thinkers were responsible for shaping their understanding of the autonomy of man and the world, and therefore for giving a peculiar character to twentieth-century "secularism." After all, it makes rather a difference when we see that the original impetus that sent the world moving in the direction of the secular was not mere indifference to religion but the propagation of specific religious world-views, world-views rejecting the Christian God in order to divinize either human reason or the process of world history. Even if it should not appear so on the surface, the chances are that, underground, the same appeal that first drew men away from Christian theism to embrace deism and pantheism is exerting its power on the imagination of "mature" man.

Nowhere, perhaps, is Bonhoeffer so prone to overlook the present influence of religion as in connection with himself and his own faith. He writes, "What we call Christianity has always been a pattern — perhaps a true pattern — of religion" (p. 162). Then he goes on to say that this era of Christianity has gone, the religious "premise" exists no more, "the linchpin is removed from the whole structure of our Christianity to date," and we can see that the Western pattern of Christianity has served as a preliminary stage to doing without religion entirely.

At the same time, he himself is continually referring for support to this very pattern. He measures his life, not alone or even chiefly by the secular months, but by the Church festivals. This is particularly evident whenever he speaks about the way in which time gains significance through personal memories and shared experience. Then, imprisonment irks him most in depriving him of physical presence in the community of Christians and such religious exercises as the hearing of sermons. Even the bitterness of separation from family and friends touches him most closely when religious celebrations would normally be the reason for their being together. Reading the Bible and regular prayers are equally taken for granted; and, though reading secular works is a great joy, these are continually discussed in the prison letters for the way in which they fit into the Christian vision of life begun in baptism and upheld through the eucharist. Indeed, the whole tone of the letters, where they are descriptive of what Bonhoeffer does and thinks, rather than concerned with generalizing about the future of Christianity, reveal a very *churchly* person as well as a very human one disliking cant and religious clichés.

It might be thought that Bonhoeffer, however, recognizes himself as one of the last survivors of an era of religion that is nearly over. Yet that hardly seems plausible, especially in the light of such a meditation as "Thoughts on the Baptism of D.W.R.," where "the piety of your home" is counted to be one of the chief blessings the baptized infant is to have for support and guidance through life. At the same time as Bonhoeffer imagines the mechanical and restrictive features in the pattern of the Christian religion to be about to pass away, he also assumes the sustaining and strengthening features are to be permanently available for the Christian.

Sometimes he almost catches himself out upholding this double estimate of religion. For example, writing of how he has found great help in Luther's advice about starting morning and evening prayers by making the sign of the cross, he adds, "Don't worry, I shan't come out of here a *homo religiosus!* On the contrary my suspicion and horror of religiosity are greater than ever" (p. 95). Obviously, this is no answer; since the more thoroughly religious an individual is the more he will detest religiosity or counterfeit, affected religion. What has to be explained is the gap between his *theory* of religionless Christianity as the style for today and tomorrow and his *practice* of Christianity incorporating so large an element of the traditional religious pattern of Western Christianity. It is true that he often found it much better to talk to honest unbelievers than to professed Christians whose "religious" talk was tainted with artificiality. Yet when he talked to these unbelievers he talked about *God.* If his objection was altogether to religion and not chiefly to a show of religion (religiosity), why was he so ready to quote biblical texts to the effect that the righteous are upheld by God? He spoke to the point when he urged that God did not exist to satisfy our needs or to rescue us from our feelings of weakness, and that Christ's salvation was not chiefly to free us from the fear of death but to fit us to face life. Yet, when the bombs were falling, he had no hesitation in quoting from Psalm 50, "Call upon me in the time of trouble: so will I hear thee and thou shalt praise me." The experience made him think of the divine judgment and "of my own unpreparedness." He sums up his feelings at those periods by saying, "But when all's said and done, it is true that it needs trouble to drive us to prayer, though every time I feel it is something to be ashamed of. Perhaps that is because up to now I have not had a chance of putting in a Christian word at such a moment" (pp. 127f.).

Discussing his slow progress in thinking out the notion of religionless Christianity, Bonhoeffer makes this interesting comment on his method of reaching conclusions: "As usual, I am led on more by an instinctive feeling for the questions which are bound to crop up rather than by any conclusions I have reached already" (p. 194). This comment should perhaps be put together with another comment, given in connection with his belief that he has never changed very much throughout his life, "Continuity with our past is a wonderful gift" (p. 159). These two confessions give us an insight into his way of thinking that is too often overlooked, namely, that he tested his theories by his total experience of faith, and never *vice versa.* His conviction that "religion is no more than the garment of Christianity" (p. 163) led him to question whether insisting that present-day Christians continue to wear the outworn garment of the Western pattern of religion might not confront us with such a problem as the early Church faced over circumcision. Just as Paul claimed that the freedom in Christ released the Christian from the bonds of the Jewish law, so the path of Christian freedom today might lead us away from the religious forms in which Christianity had been presented during the "ages of religion." Taking an outside view, however, we can see that Bonhoeffer's very demand for a casting aside of the old religious garment was in continuity with his particular religious tradition. His polemic against identifying the gospel with a metaphysical understanding of God was in line with Luther's polemic against using "carnal reason" in the realm of faith, and his denunciation of religiosity was an updating of Luther's thinking on the "Babylonian captivity of the Church," in which institutional religion negates the freedom of the Christian man by setting itself up above the gospel that calls us to the obedience of faith and the service of our fellows.

Because he rested firmly in the continuity provided by his Lutheran past, Bonhoeffer was able to trust his instinctive feelings about the questions that were important to ask at any particular moment in history, setting little store by his interim answers to date. During his last days he eagerly followed one set of questions and pursued the line of religionless Christianity with typical enthusiasm and earnestness. No doubt he would have dropped his tentative conclusions along that line, had he lived to see that the future was not, after all, to be so religionless as he had imagined. The Luther he loved to quote used to say that man cannot know a "naked God," and Bonhoeffer's own faith (as we can see so clearly at this distance from him) was never anything approaching a "naked faith" stripped from its religious garment. Yet, if he underestimated his involvement in a particular pattern of religion that was so much a part of him that he took it for granted and never saw it, he was right in insisting that we must know that redemption lies in God's grace in Jesus Christ and never religion as such.

He was right too in his estimate of the Christian's freedom to accept responsible life in the world, and in his insistence that a cure for God-forgetfulness cannot be found by way of a return to the tutelage of a religious-centered culture. In his *Ethics* there is an analysis of two strands in modern secular culture, one an acceptance of the natural dimension of life which does not deny the Creator of all life, and the other which, seeking power over the world, loses itself in a lust for power that inevitably culminates in nihilism. This double view of "worldliness," perhaps unfortunately, does not appear in *Letters and Papers from Prison,* except in an occasional (and unexplained) reference to nihilism. At the same time, Bonhoeffer does refer to his view that the Christian must be aware of the vital distinction between the "ultimate" and the "penultimate" in life. Although immersed in "worldly" living, the Christian has to maintain a "secret discipline" apart from the world's view, in order to keep alive his understanding that the penultimate of activity is not the whole of existence. One passage in *Letters and Papers* puts his conviction about the wholeness of life, ultimate and penultimate conjoined yet not confused, in the form of an analogy drawn from music:

> There is always a danger of intense love destroying what I might call the 'polyphony' of life. What I mean is that God requires that we should love him eternally with our whole hearts, yet not so as to compromise or diminish our earthly affections, but as a kind of *cantus firmus* to which the other melodies of life provide the counterpoint. Earthly affection is one of those contrapuntal themes, a theme which enjoys an autonomy of its own. . . . Where the ground bass is firm and clear, there is nothing to stop the counterpoint from being developed to the utmost of its limits. . . . I wanted to tell you that we must have a good, clear *cantus firmus.* Without it there can be no full or perfect sound, but with it the counterpoint has a firm support and cannot get out of tune or fade out, yet is always a perfect whole in its own right. Only a polyphony of this kind can give life wholeness, and at the same time assure us that nothing can go wrong so long as the *cantus firmus* is kept going (pp. 175f.).

What Bonhoeffer certainly grasped in his own experience, but failed to make plain as a guiding rule for preserving the universal polyphony of life, is that to keep the *cantus firmus* going, human beings need the support of a guiding pattern of religion. Speaking in one place of how shallow and purposeless modern life has become when men have no better stimulus than "sentimental radio 'hits'" to foster their spiritual efforts, he adds, "I have long had a special affection for the season between Easter and Ascension Day. . . . How can men endure earthly tensions if they know nothing of the tension between earth and heaven?" (p. 157). How indeed? But without a religious pattern that provides us with *religious* festivals inviting us to meditate upon the tension between earth and heaven, are we likely to withdraw our gaze from the penultimate in order to contemplate the ultimate?

Religion may be only a garment. Nevertheless, human beings assert their humanity by wearing clothes and reflect their sense of values in the clothes they choose. The unclothed state of religionless Christianity is an abstract possibility, and a practical nonpossibility. Clothes do not make the man (though Carlyle in his *Sartor Resartus* had a point). They may help him to remember that he is one, and that as such he is more than a child of this world. The parable of the man who was cast out from the wedding feast because he was not wearing the appropriate garment (Matt. 22:11-14) may have an uncanny relevance to our contemporary cultural situation.

Part 4

ABOUT THE SECULAR IN FAITH AND MORALS

NINE

THE SECULAR MADE SACRED

As I walked through the wilderness of this world....
— *John Bunyan,* The Pilgrim's Progress

If the word "new" is the operative word today in connection with Christianity, the word "secular" has become the glamour word. To use it shows that the user knows what really is *in,* and that the word "religious" is completely *out.* The number of theological books with "secular" in the title seems now to outstrip the number featuring "new." One has the feeling that people who have little interest in Christianity or in faith in general, and have been getting along very well without giving too much thought to the matter, must be rather puzzled by all the theologians who are so anxious to tell them that they are living in an age of radical secularity. Like Monsieur Jourdain in Molière's *Le Bourgeois Gentilhomme,* whose teachers informed him that he had been speaking prose all his life without knowing it, they must conclude that expert knowledge is a wonderful thing. Though it is possible that, unless they share the naiveté of Molière's famous character, they may not be entirely so excited by the news as he was.

It is also possible that there may be a certain naiveté exhibited on the part of the would-be teachers. It is one thing to use a word and another thing to use it unequivocally, making the word mean exactly what it seems to mean. Applying the word "new" to a noun does not necessarily result in cancelling the noun's connections with the old, and so it is with the word "secular" and the religious. We must always remember that the secular and the sacred (or religious) are linked terms,

91

not contradictories. They belong together. Nobody ordinarily speaks of anything being secular unless he has at the back or the front of his mind the thought that it *could be* religious. No scientist would dream of saying, "I am going to conduct a secular experiment," and no cook would announce, "One medium-rare secular steak coming up!" "Will you join us in some purely secular conversation?" is a possible question; but the person addressed would no doubt be a minister or priest. In fact, to call *this, that,* and *the other,* a secular *this,* a secular *that,* and a secular *other,* is really a very religious thing to do.

The reason why is not far to seek. It is because in the secular-sacred scale the secular is fixed by reference to the sacred and not *vice versa.* Historically, the sacred is first separated out and everything else lumped together as the "profane." So when the distinction between the secular and the religious appears, the secular is simply the religious man's estimate of the sphere outside the specifically religious sphere in which he himself operates; it is the "worldly" as opposed to the "spiritual" realm. But that does not mean that he views it as independent of religion — quite the reverse. He regards it naturally as territory which is in principle subject to "spiritual" rule, and which is allowed only that freedom religion permits it to retain.

This history cannot be shaken off. Whenever anyone says anything about the secular (even if it is the dogmatic pronouncement, "There is nothing *except* the secular!") he speaks with a religious accent and affirms that he stands upon the ground of the sacred. Thus a "secular Christianity" cannot but be the creation of a religious piety, however much disguised. Just as refusing to speak about God does not make a theologian's theology actually godless, so insisting that his outlook is a secular one does not sever a theologian from his concern with the area of religion. To imagine it could do this would be to cultivate that kind of simplicity which takes at face value the illusionist's assurance that he has nothing up his sleeve. If we believe him, sooner or later we shall experience disillusionment.

Theologies of the secular-Christian type antedate death-of-God theologies, since they can claim direct inspiration from Bonhoeffer, whereas the warrant in Bonhoeffer for Christian atheism is less immediately apparent. Nevertheless, there is a good deal of affinity between the two; and it would seem that the advent of the latter has given fresh impetus to the former, so that as soon as Christian atheism hit the inevitable slump following every *succès de scandale,* secular Christianity seemed to take on new life.

The atheistic motif in secular Christianity is much more restrained than that which presses its way into the central place in death-of-God theologies. Bonhoeffer's explanation that God had allowed himself to be edged out of the world is the usual starting-point for secular-Christian theologies. This leaves the initiative still with God, whereas the demand of Christian atheism that the Christian should will the death of God snatches all power of decision from the divine and transfers it to the human. Nevertheless, the logic of secular Christianity demands the latter also. Thus van Buren's argument that the need for consistency within a secularist outlook compels us to excise the word "God" from our human vocabulary shows the point at which the two ways of thinking agree and converge. Other types of secular Christianity advocate instead a restrained silence in connection with speaking about God, as though the bounds of secular good taste would be broken if we were ever to refer too openly to the divine. But, of course, equivocation in the name of modest reticence cannot be maintained indefinitely. If secular Christianity is prepared, in the last resort, to do without a genuinely transcendent God by refusing to name him, then what god does its secularist "theology" propose to put in his place? What is the pattern of religion it lives by that enables it to speak of the secular world instead of the world *tout court?*

The answer to that question is supplied quite readily in the account secular Christianity gives of itself.

Among recent books on the secular meaning of the gospel none has had more effect than Harvey Cox's *The Secular City.* The popular success it has achieved might just possibly substantiate my point that the word "secular" is even more potent at the moment than the word "new," since *The Secular City,* appearing in 1965, seems to have caught people's imagination more than Gibson Winter's *The New Creation as Metropolis* published two years earlier. Cox's work is extremely readable and also very wide-ranging. It lays down a theoretical basis for a viable secular Christianity and then proceeds to show how the theory can be directly applied to contemporary society. It shows an ample familiarity with the most recent relevant literature on the subject. It abounds with down-to-earth observations about the passing scene. It is shrewd and tough-minded. And it holds our attention by its ongoing argument, while it delights us by its asides.

Cox starts out to present an explanation of secularization that shall throw light upon Bonhoeffer's concept of man's coming of age. He does so by drawing upon Friedrich Gogarten's thesis that secularization is a late-dawning effect of Christian faith (a thesis recently interpreted for Anglo-Saxon readers in Larry Shiner's 1966 book on Gogarten, *The Secularization of History*), and upon the thought of the contemporary Dutch theologian C. A. van Peursen. His initial assumption is that "religion and metaphysical versions of Christianity" are "becoming more peripheral," so that we have no choice except to "let go and immerse ourselves in the new world of the secular city" (p. 3). *Urbanization* is the great new fact of our time. If we happen to be Christians, we must accept our new urban home, not *although* but more especially *because* we so call ourselves.

Cox next argues that the intrinsic compatibility between Christianity and secularization has its roots in the Bible. Secularization means in its early stages the *desacralization,* first of nature, and subsequently of politics. The biblical story of creation and the account of the nationhood of Israel being achieved at the exodus from Egypt show us these two processes successfully carried through. At creation man is placed in the world God has given him as his own to oversee; and, in being set free from Pharaoh's rule, Israel is made accountable to God alone and sent out into history and social change.

The first event shows that nature is not itself divine. Man, if he is to find God, must find him in free obedience. The second event shows that there is no divinely ordained social order. Man does not owe religious obedience to a divine priest-king, but society is organized for the well-being of man and the right ordering of his community lies within man's own

94

decision. The two together indicate that the biblical understanding of life in the world establishes a patent fact: *the cosmos is secularized.* This fact implies that the Christian who accepts the biblical view fully can never place "religion" above "the world" as a higher reality. A further implication of the discovery of a secularized cosmos must be understood also, namely, *all human values are relativized.* The biblical warrant for this additional insight is located in the prohibition of idolatry. Since man is not to worship anything that he himself can make, it must be obvious that idolatry is not merely limited to worshipping graven images. Worshipping (i.e. counting as divine) human ideas, philosophies, or value-systems must be counted equally to fall under that which God forbids when he forbids us to manufacture gods from the things of earth.

Cox witnesses to some important elements in the Bible. The Genesis account of creation certainly affirms that the Creator cannot be identified with his creation or any part of it. The Exodus account of the deliverance of Israel from the power of Egypt certainly affirms that the Creator's power is demonstrated in history and is neither delegated permanently to any ruler or priest, nor tied to any holy place. But this is surely not everything contained in these two Old Testament books that still is of relevance today. The omissions in Cox's review of what the biblical record has to say about the relation of man to God are glaring. He gives the creation story without the fall, and Israel's calling as a nation without the call of Abraham. And, lacking these, the record is thrown out of balance, and therefore falsified. Because the elements of scriptural truth Cox isolates are so far from being the whole truth, the end result is something totally unbiblical.

Biblical faith, Cox avers, desacralizes the cosmos. For the cosmos to be desacralized, however, it must first have become sacralized. How did this happen? Cox assumes that we must approach the question through the history of mankind's evolving religious consciousness. At first, men developed religions that conceived the gods to be resident in nature. Then, in the history of the Hebrew people, an advance was made when the God of Israel was divorced from nature by being lifted "above" it. This laid the foundation for the advent of secularization when the human race reached the maturity of consciousness that it has achieved today.

Cox's approach here is difficult to relate to the Bible, which does not give its answers on the level of human consciousness but on the level of the human response to the divine revelation. Man, made in the image of God, was made for communion with God. The fall broke the relationship on man's side. The result is that fallen man, left to himself, does not recognize God, honor him, or give him thanks, and has exchanged the truth about God accessible to him into a lie, worshipping the creature rather than the Creator (Rom. 1:18-24). God, nevertheless, has not left man to himself. The scriptural record is the record of God's initiative in reversing the effects of the fall.

Again, looking at the exodus of Israel from Egypt, Cox sees the beginning of a process whereby human consciousness has become weaned from the notion of the sacred in persons or places, a process continued by the protests of the prophets against idolatry in every form, and completed in our own day by the vanishing of religion as such. Having reached the stage of a completely secularized society, we have to rid ourselves of the last vestiges of superstitious reliance upon any imagined power "above" the world. We must discover God in the world engaged in "making and keeping life human" by becoming his partners, and, in this way, fulfilling the purpose for which we were created. Such a view of the significance of the exodus, however, seems to have very slight contact with the Book of Exodus, which relates the power of God in freeing Israel from the Egyptians to the purpose of God in creating a holy people on the basis of his promise to Abraham. And it equally ignores the New Testament description of the Church as the New Israel, which is, no less than the Old Israel, a holy people set apart from "the world." What Cox sees in the Church of the New Testament, under the guidance of the contemporary German sociologist Dietrich von Oppen, is the first glimpse of the "organization principle" in Western history (pp. 152-155). Because Christians became members of the new community by a personal decision that usually meant cutting across family, religious, or ethnic relationships, we see here the beginning of a truly human development of freedom-in-decision through which man became enabled to choose "his own associations and his own life-style."

What is remarkable about Cox's reading of the Bible in developmental and sociological terms is its single-mindedness. Cox never seems to consider that, even if the Bible provides us with insights into the development of the history of religions and allows us to trace some of the (partial?) sources of later sociological developments, the possibility of finding these insights and these historical sources may not be the sole reward we reap for opening the Bible.

The only really possible explanation of Cox's peculiar way of handling biblical material is to say that he is interested in what the Bible says only when it can be made to justify the style of life evident in contemporary secular society. Everything else — and in particular the whole biblical emphasis that the sacred dimension of life has its source in a holy God who demands holiness and passes judgment upon all that is unholy — is pushed aside. In spite of everything Cox says about the need to relativize all human values, there is one value he tacitly accepts as absolute and uses to establish his positive estimate of secularity. This is the value of human responsibility for himself and the world — man's world, the only world there is! — when that responsibility is sole and unshared. Cox's position is not merely that on the whole the gains in secularity outweigh the disadvantages. He assumes it to be the one way forward, the unambiguous expression of true human creativity. Living out that creativity is the incarnation of true faith, experiencing now participation in the transcendent,

> And one far-off divine event
> To which the whole creation moves.

In other words, Cox uses the Bible, history, and sociology as grist for the mill of the theory of religion he has espoused. Because this is so, he has no trouble at all in finding the right "non-religious interpretation of biblical concepts" that Bonhoeffer never discovered. For him "interpretation" means simple translation of love of God into love of city. One just shifts the biblical concepts in order to focus them on an earthly instead of on a supernatural subject. One just converts the concept of conversion, for example, into accepting responsibility

97

in the secular city. It is as simple as that, although old-fashioned people might call it idolatry.

Cox's theory is, in its essentials, that of Auguste Comte, the nineteenth-century French philosopher who believed that there were three stages to be discerned in human consciousness: the mythical, the metaphysical, and the "positive" or scientific. Comte advocated, as the human response to the development of man's consciousness of the world, the establishment of a nonsupernatural religion of humanity. Cox is as eager as Comte to put away all vestiges of the mythical and metaphysical world-views (he is emphatic that metaphysics has disappeared as entirely from our secular style of life as has religion) so that we may commit ourselves to the third stage. Yet he cannot, using the terms he has adopted, admit that he wants a religion of humanity. The nearest he comes to saying what he does want is in his Afterword in the volume *The Secular City Debate,* where he writes, "Man, seen as the steersman of the cosmos, is the only starting point we have for a viable doctrine of God" (p. 199).

Seemingly, Cox presents us with yet another version of the religion where God is identified with process. He tells us in *The Secular City,* "When we look at history as a process of secularization, it becomes for us at the same time meaningful *and* open-ended" (p. 94). Of course, a process that is closed is dead, no longer a process at all except in memory. It is futile to speculate about the end of any process, for all we can say is that it is proceeding. The most we can do is to observe the present direction of the process and report what we are seeing now, which suggests the probable course of the immediate future, provided no unforeseen new developments occur. But we can always look back and say something about the previous history of the process. And this is exactly what Cox does. He tells us of the past that is gone for ever and directs us to look at what the process has come up with lately. The process, he assures us, has left behind myth and metaphysics, and is moving at present into secularity. But it has also moved from a world uniting small units to a much more complex world of large units, forcing life from the country, village, and town to the modern city, which he christens *technopolis.* The process has come up with the secular city, and it is here that we must look for a revelation of what the process will allow us to believe and how it commands us to behave.

The secular city, Cox tells us, is a "viable concretization of the ancient symbol of the Kingdom of God" (p. 98). First, the secular city, like the Kingdom of God disclosed by the coming of Jesus, represents a partnership between God and man. Second, the secular city, like the Kingdom of God preached by Jesus, requires renunciation and penitence as we leave old values and loyalties at the appearance of a new reality. Third, the secular city, like the Kingdom of God which some biblical scholars describe as an eschatology *in process of realizing itself* (italics his), is present to us as a demand and a challenge to take up a new life.

This identification of the secular city with the Kingdom of God looks like a fantastic joke, yet Cox takes it with the utmost seriousness. It cannot even be supposed that for him the secular city symbolizes the Kingdom, for he deliberately puts it the other way round, saying that the symbol of the Kingdom is concretely manifest in the secular city. Roman Catholic theology has been wont to insist that the Church, because it is the visible expression of the Kingdom, must always be given the title of Holy Church. It would make things perfectly clear and free from inconsistency were Cox to follow this line of thought and name his secular city the Holy City. After all, in his estimate the secular city takes over the full role of being the essential mediator between God and man. Here it is that the promise of new life is graciously offered; here that penitence is demanded; and here that conversion leads to new freedom and a hope that cannot fade or die. Outside the secular city there is no salvation for modern man.

In point of fact, it is difficult to believe that Cox's phrase *the secular city* can have any intelligible meaning unless it is that of the Holy City, New Jerusalem, after the model of the city described in the Book of Revelation, the city that comes down out of heaven from God (Rev. 21:2). Can one conceive of a "real place" actually being called the secular city? It is possible to imagine an old-time atheist having given this name to a town he founded, as a public testimony to his desire to see in being an enlightened metropolis free from the blight of religious teaching and preaching. If it is still around, this hypothetical city will by now have its standard quota of churches, meeting-houses, and headquarters of esoteric cults, and it will probably be in line for playing host to the General Assembly of the World Council of Churches sometime next century. But unlike any city we know, the New Jerusalem of the Apocalypse has no temple. There is no holy place there because there is no need to mark off its religious life from its civic life. Nothing in the city can be termed either sacred or profane. The difference between the New Jerusalem and Cox's secular city is that the one comes down from heaven and the other grows — unfriendly critics would say "sprawls" — upon earth. The vital distinction between the two is that Cox's secular city is in process. So, although God is in it (and for that reason we can be sure that religion, together with metaphysics, is "disappearing for ever"), he is not yet entirely in it. Consequently, we have still great difficulty in naming him. He hides himself in the future. Bonhoeffer believed that the coming of secularity might clear the decks for the God of the Bible. Cox believes that the proclamation of the death of God — that is, the "static" God who "is" and now "was" — "may clear the decks for the God who *will be*" (*The Secular City Debate*, pp. 202-3. Cox's italics).

Cox attempts to tie his notion of the God-who-will-be to the Bible by referring to "He who cometh." But this is a sophistry. The King who was proclaimed as coming when Jesus entered Jerusalem was both visible and known by his name. He is the one who declares himself through the Spirit to the churches to be the first and the last and the living one, who died and is alive for ever (Rev. 1:17, 18). It is very noticeable throughout Cox's work that the knowledge Paul considered to be the sole essential knowledge is apparently not worth knowing in the secular city: Jesus Christ — Christ nailed to the cross (1 Cor. 2:2). In an unfallen world, in process of realizing itself in order to reveal the God-who-will-be, Jesus as the Lamb of God, he who takes away the sin of the world (John 1:29), is superfluous. The significance of Jesus is that he calls men away from old religious loyalties and values, and gives witness to the love and service of man as the central concern of human existence.

Penitence, to be sure, is needed, for the secular city demands it. But the quality of this penitence is the realization that we have refused the new values necessary for giving wholehearted service to the secular city. (Our service, it should be noted, is service *to* the city, as to our proper Lord. Why religion is to be rejected is chiefly because it distracts us from our obedience to the call of the city by the illusion that there is something "above" the city of equal or greater worth. While we retain any religion we try, faithlessly, to serve two masters.) There is also warfare to be conducted against evil, or at least against obstructions to achieving our goals. Cox identifies these obstructions with the biblical "principalities and powers." These powers, he tells us, "actually signify all the forces in a culture which cripple and corrupt human freedom" (*The Secular City*, p. 110). It seems, however, that we shall overcome such powers when we know that the message the Christian Church has to proclaim is that "the One who frees slaves and summons men to maturity is still in business" (p. 110). The knowledge we require is knowledge of our ability to draw on the truth "that man not only *should* but also *can* have dominion over the earth!" (p. 112). The Christian message is not one of our need of redemption, and the fact of redemption in the cross of Christ, but the fact of our freedom and our need to know that we can exercise that freedom.

Since he conceives creation without the fall, Cox imagines "partnership with God" to be a sufficient Christian description of human existence. He reads the acts of God in history as being everything that increases human freedom, and calls us to throw our weight energetically at every place where God can be seen working his work of liberation. He writes, "Jesus calls men to adulthood, a condition in which they are freed from their bondage to the infantile images of the species and of the self" (p. 134). Most Christians have imagined up to now that Jesus called men to repent. And the Old Testament prophets saw the acts of God in judgments that were as often restricting (going into exile) or catastrophic (defeat in war) as liberating. To take up our cross and become a disciple may be freedom from infantile images, but it is not obviously that; and the call to discipleship is more likely to look to us like "the most fiendish cruelty," as Kierkegaard said Christianity must look where the fact of sin and the necessity of deliverance from guilt are not recognized.

To become fellow-workers with God is the call of God to man, but only when man is in a position to hear and obey God's call. That is why the biblical message is, from first to last, a message of the need for repentance and the call to faith. Without doubt the gospel according to Cox is, from first to last, a gospel of good works. Faith of a kind is needed, namely, faith in our unrealized potentialities to be finally revealed by the God-who-will-be. This faith is based on evidence of past advances into freedom seen in Judeo-Christian history. Cox explains, "Exodus and Easter remain the two foci of biblical faith, the basis on which the theology of the church must be developed" (p. 114). Exodus shows us God liberating his people from bondage, and Easter that the same liberating activity goes on today. The upshot of it all is that man must take responsibility "in and for the city of man." The Christian Church's task in the process is to take up the extra good work of being "God's *avant-garde*" for the sake of the secular city, in the service of which is perfect freedom.

Now, there is no reason why the Christian Church should not be God's *avant-garde;* and several good reasons why it should, among these being the direction of its Lord that his disciples ought to do more than others (Matt. 5:47). The relevant question, though, is whether the Church can be the Church without also believing more than others. And, in this connection, it is odd that Cox should ask us to look within *biblical* history for evidence of the liberating process in history. If the only reason for looking back to a religious tradition — one that used to call on God and think of him as the judge of men's sins and the source of their salvation — is to be thankful that we are now free from the religious preoccupations of that tradition, why look to it in the first place? Certainly, on Cox's reading, this religious tradition bred within itself a cure for its own disease, for it eventually secularized itself. But long before the Judeo-Christian tradition began to be secularized, the Greek philosopher Protagoras affirmed the great secular axiom that man is the measure of all things. Why seek the secular among the religious, when the secular has already arisen elsewhere?

Plainly, Cox looks back to biblical history and speaks about developing a theology of the Church because his concern is, first and last, with religion. Why he does not call his concern by this

102

name is that he reserves the word "religion" for the supernatural interpretation of the world that now, he believes, is being replaced by a nonsupernatural or "nonreligious" interpretation. Nevertheless, an authentically secular outlook would be one that, by definition, excluded all traffic with Bible, theology, and Church. Cox can assume that the old supernatural Christianity and the new secular Christianity are in essential continuity only when he makes the further assumption that the secular stance at last lays bare the *real* meaning of Christianity, that is, discloses the true world-view answering our unsolved problem concerning the ultimate meaning of life. In other words, supernatural Christianity was a religion fitting the needs of times of ignorance; secular Christianity is a religion fitting the times of maturity. Secularity clears a space for religion in a world that does not recognize anything "higher" than man. Exit, then, supernaturalistic faith. Enter Comte's religion of humanity, renamed "secular Christianity."

Here, once more, we see a "theology" that seeks to imitate Bonhoeffer's acceptance of the world that has come of age but reverses Bonhoeffer's approach, losing the latter's belief that "we can make room in our hearts, to some extent at least, for God and the whole world" (*Letters and Papers,* p. 189). Bonhoeffer insisted that life must be kept "multidimensional" and "polyphonous." A secular faith that thinks it must exclude anything that does not fit within the secular dimension denies at the outset the *cantus firmus* that, for Bonhoeffer, permits the polyphony to be developed to the full. Such a restricted faith is happy to live *without* God, but makes no sense out of living *before* God, and still less of living with "the great concepts of Christian theology."

The real inspiration for the secular Christian theories adopted by Cox and others is the line of thinking opened up by Friedrich Gogarten. Gogarten's thesis is that secularity is to be distinguished from secularism. The former is a direct, if long-delayed, effect of biblical Christianity. The latter is a dogmatic faith, denying the Christian perspective upon the secular. (Cox develops Gogarten's thesis in the first chapter of *The Secular City.*) What is overlooked here is that the notion of secularity arose out of the separation of the secular from the religious and the belief that man finds his proper freedom in cultivating the secular at the expense of the religious. Secularity, therefore, can only be a stage in the drive towards secularism. Secularity is content to concentrate upon the world without God, believing that the sphere of religion takes care of God-talk. It is a short step from that belief to denial of the utility of the religious sphere completely and to absolutizing the secular by adopting the dogma of secularism.

There cannot be a theology of the secular. But there can be a theology of the natural. In his last book, incomplete and published after his death, the *Ethics* (1955, English ed.), Bonhoeffer partly developed such a theology. For him the natural is never self-sufficient and assumes that all life stands under God. In the sphere of nature man finds a relative independence and a relative freedom with regard to his neighbor. He writes, "But it is of crucial importance that this relative freedom shall not be confused with an absolute freedom for God and one's neighbor such as only the imparted word of God itself can create and bestow" (p. 102).

Neglect of the last consideration accounts for one of the obvious, and frequently remarked on, defects of Cox's secular Christianity. By identifying (in principle) the secular city with the Kingdom of God, Cox seems to forsake realism for a starry-eyed, romantic glorification of city life. He might have done well to heed Bonhoeffer's reminder, "The Bible tells us that Cain was the first city dweller" (*Letters and Papers*, p. 182). Cox is surely right, nevertheless, in telling us that the advent of technopolis is not only an irreversible fact but also a development calculated to bring a richer life to humanity as a whole. Where Cox's enthusiasm seems to shade into propaganda is where he goes on to suggest that not only must we accept technopolis as a present fact, and work to make it an instrument for human well-being, but also forsake all other loyalties to serve it. The cause of this idolatry of the secular city is rooted in his neglect of the doctrine of the fall of man, and his consequent failure to place man and all his works under the judgment of God.

The city provides, as Cox points out, a symbol, if not *the* symbol, of the complete realization of the Kingdom of God. The biblical New Jerusalem, Augustine's City of God, and Bunyan's Celestial City witness to this truth. Yet Cox strangely omits to tell us that the city provides equally a symbol of the power of evil organized in defiance of God. It is Nineveh, Babylon, and the City of Dreadful Night. The city, whatever form it may take — and it is always taking new forms, so that Cox's emphasis upon the utter novelty of technopolis is both correct and misleading — is at once a monument to man's hope for human brotherhood and to his cruel betrayal of his brother. In *The City of God* Augustine pointed out that the Roman story of Romulus and Remus, as well as the Bible, links the founding of the city with fratricide, in this way recognizing how all community created by man begins in blood guilt and how the innocent can have no continuing city on earth but find their citizenship beyond the earth.

Rejecting the supernatural as merely an outmoded worldview, Cox fails to see that antisupernaturalism in the form of belief in an open-ended process is no less a world-view; and it happens also to be a world-view excluding the living (and not just the metaphysical) transcendence of God. In the one-dimensional world of process, no recognition is given to the radical ambiguity of all human efforts, including city-building. Thus a dogmatic theology of process, demanding present unconditional service to a city of human values, overlooks what plain common sense sees well enough: the city's ultimate foundation in brute force. It does not face the fact that, while the city of man is not without justice and even love, it conceives its first duty to be survival. It lives from a power basis that will not hesitate to break all laws, both human and divine, to maintain or further itself. It will make a ruin of the earth before it will surrender its life.

If we are lucky (which means, in mid-twentieth-century North America, if we are middle-class and preferably white), we may find the City of Man a pleasant place in which to live. If we are clever (and technology is making us more clever every day), we may yet plan ourselves into some kind of Utopia, though whether that will be a heavenly or a hellish existence we may perhaps not be able to tell by the time we reach it if, as they must, brainwashing techniques improve. The arrival of Utopia might well coincide with the moment we decide to annihilate the earth, thus founding the new City of Tomorrow (on another planet?) by a new dimension of fratricide.

We would be wise to leave prophecy about the City of

105

Tomorrow to science fiction. Our concern is with the City of To-day, which is the City of Man. Assuredly not the secular city, the City of Man is rather a secularistic city inhabited by people with no one dominant religion, and many new religions being present-ly proposed. The human work that we can do in the city we ought to do as well as we can, but we should never be deluded into thinking that this is the substance of our Christian witness, though it may well be its form. However it is expressed, our witness must be to the God who *is* and to his Christ, while we look forward "to the city with firm foundations, whose architect and builder is God" (Heb. 11:10).

Today Christian faith is likely to say, as Bonhoeffer said in his day, "Never have we realized, as we do to-day, how the world lies under the wrath and grace of God" (p. 183). And it will add, with him, "May God in his mercy lead us through these times. But above all may he lead us to himself!" (p. 227).

TEN

NEW MORALITY

Our acts our angels are, or good or ill,
Our fatal shadows that walk by us still.
— Francis Beaumont and John Fletcher,
Upon an Honest Man's Fortune

When you have a New Theology on your hands you soon
have a New Morality as well. Religion and standards of conduct
go together; a change in one indicates a change in the other.
Religion says first, "So believe!" and next, "So do!" The Old
Testament has its Ten Commandments — and many more rules.
The New Testament has its Sermon on the Mount — and many
more precepts. The infallibility of the Pope is declared to extend
equally to matters of faith and matters of morals.

It should be noted, though, that the link is between religion
and *standards* of conduct, not necessarily between religion and
good conduct. The religious person seeks so to behave as to
please God, but the kind of behavior resulting depends on the
kind of his religion. In some religions it is considered more important to kill the unbelieving enemy than to help the believing
brother; and, in most, the obligation to perform the recognized
rituals is placed above the obligation to public or private
morality. A man of almost any faith can recognize himself in
the old story of the pious storekeeper who called downstairs to
his son, "Have you sanded the sugar? Have you watered the milk?
Then come up to prayers!"

Even when a religion puts morality right at its heart, it still
cannot think of anything being really good unless it is divinely
revealed and divinely commanded:

> *He has showed you, O man, what is good;*
> *and what does the Lord require of you*
> *but to do justice, and to love kindness,*
> *and to walk humbly with your God?*
> *(Micah 6:8)*

Our being good to others is required, not first for the sake of goodness, but to prove our obedience. We follow where God leads. Love of God and love of man are joined in the Great Commandment of Jesus (Mark 12:29); but here, too, love of man comes specifically marked "second." Most theologians uphold the view that a thing is good because God wills it rather than that God wills it because it is good. Only a theology strongly influenced by philosophy — Thomism for instance — is willing to consider the alternative view.

Since the religious person thinks that his first duty is to obey the divine commands, his outlook is at odds with that of the ethical thinker, whose task is to look into the nature of goodness itself. Unless ethics is associated from the start with religious faith, goodness "for its own sake" is interpreted universally as meaning "for the sake of man." So it is not unnatural for some ethical thinkers to think they have a duty to attack religion, or for some antireligionists to take up ethical thinking. When believers and unbelievers argue about conduct, each side usually blames the other for being immoral. The believers say that without religion everyone is free to please himself, leaving nothing to stop everybody from indulging in the most fearful crimes. The unbelievers retort that religious bigotry is the biggest single obstacle in the path of moral reform, and that there is nothing particularly moral about obeying laws out of fear that God will strike you down if you don't please him.

In a way, both parties to this dispute are right. They both want good standards upheld in society, but the first is thinking of good *standards,* and the second of *good* standards. In other words, it is more important for the man of religion to be sure that he has definite obligations than to be able to demonstrate exactly how fulfilling these obligations contributes to human welfare. If he is convinced that the will of God demands anything, he assumes it must be something good. On the other hand, the ethical thinker wants to know that an act is good — and why — before he feels he has any obligation to perform it. What

108

he values most is freedom to judge for himself; whereas the man of religion believes the best choice is to choose the path of obedience. Christian theology finds the highest freedom in the state of grace, or spontaneously accepting God's will, instead of accepting grudgingly, which is living by the law. But, in any case, God chooses the rules by which his universe is governed. To wish to make our own is not freedom but self-destructive self-will.

Whenever there are changes in the rules by which religious people live, this is clear evidence that religious belief is changing. At the very least, the will of God is being differently interpreted, and this may indicate that former beliefs about the nature of God himself are being jettisoned. From the angle of the man-in-the-street, it is easier to see what kinds of changes are going on in religious belief by noting alterations in what is religiously permitted or prohibited than by attending to theological explanations. Considered strictly in terms of theology, for example, the question "Is God dead?" is far more urgent than "Is adultery a sin?" For, if the first question is answered affirmatively, the second has been effectively ruled out. Yet a magazine article headed "Is Adultery a Sin?" is likely to have readers long after articles asking "Is God Dead?" have ceased to stir interest. It will not matter greatly, either, whether the article about adultery takes a "liberal" view or argues on conventional grounds for keeping adultery a sin. Either way, a doubt has been raised about the previously accepted rule that adultery is contrary to the will of God. So even to ask the question is to be provocative, suggesting that all religious beliefs are in the melting-pot.

Largely because of the New Morality's apparent readiness to relax the traditional Christian veto on extramarital sex acts, it has attracted widespread attention, and also gained the name of the New Immorality. Yet, even at the level of popular journalism, there is some recognition of the fact that more important issues are being raised in talk of a New Morality than merely second thoughts on a single moral question. Some New Moralists have claimed that what the New Morality really seeks is a new moral vigor and incisiveness among Christians. The New Morality is determined to grapple seriously with Christian decisions of all kinds, especially in connection with such urgent contemporary questions as race relations and war. However, there

109

seems to be even more at stake than a new look at how to apply Christianity to the modern world. The New Morality has raised the fundamental issue of whether rules are vital for a healthy morality, and thus whether the traditional religious approach — meaning the traditional Christian approach in particular — is any longer viable. The New Morality suggests that the religious concern with fixed standards of conduct ought to give way to a concern with *good* conduct.

For example, Robinson's chapter on "The New Morality" (he puts the title within quotation marks) in *Honest To God* contains the following explanation:

> For nothing can of itself always be labelled as "wrong." One cannot, for instance, start from the position "sex relations before marriage" or "divorce" are wrong or sinful in themselves. They may be in 99 cases or even 100 cases out of a hundred, but they are not intrinsically so, for the only intrinsic evil is lack of love (p. 118).

Robinson observes that traditional Christian opinion will be incensed by such an approach to thinking about morals. He is right, of course. Those concentrating on the particular moral question cited will at once see the thin-edge-of-the-wedge maneuvering in the bishop's example. If you can come down that hypothetical one percent from 100 to 99, they will say, you may later decide that it is right to come down another one percent, then fifty percent, and end by advocating complete sexual anarchy. But this is not the point, though it is a point that may justly be made, incidentally. The point is that, even granted the bishop's figure of 100 cases out of a hundred, rules have been brushed out of the path and, with them, any objective standard of right and wrong. *There is, in Robinson's view, no intrinsic evil apart from lack of love.* And love, we know, cannot be subjected to rules.

The consequences of admitting Robinson's proposition, which I have put in a negative form for emphasis, is what this chapter will try to examine.

But first I should like to follow up what I have been saying about the New Morality's opposition to deciding moral problems by way of fixing standards by means of rules. In taking up this position and arguing that what matters is *good* conduct (or *loving* conduct), supporters of the New Morality seem to

110

have come over to the side of those who in the past opposed putting morality under the authority of religion, arguing that morality is its own warrant. Good is good and right is right, and bringing in the will of God neither makes a bad act good nor shows right conduct to be one iota more right. In other words, by saying that modern Christians no longer look to the will of God for deciding how they themselves should act or how they should judge the actions of others, the New Morality proves itself to be secular Christianity applied to the ethical field.

Now, my conclusion about secular Christianity was that it claimed to be nonreligious, but actually behaved as a religion. If this conclusion is more than arbitrary, it ought to follow that the New Morality seems to be looking at the field of ethics from a nonreligious perspective, and that it seems to be concerned with *good* conduct, and not primarily with standards — certainly not with fixed rules. But only *"seems."* Actually (again, if I am on the right track) the New Morality goes against its claims by setting up a standard, by invoking rules, and by behaving in a thoroughly "religious" fashion, yet not in the fashion of historic Christianity. I shall look at one prominent example of the New Morality, as set out by Joseph Fletcher, in order to see whether my hypothesis about the religious quality of the "secular Christian ethic" can be substantiated.

Situation Ethics: The New Morality by Joseph Fletcher appeared in 1966, but Fletcher's approach to Christian ethics — he refused to call it a system — had already been hailed by Robinson in *Honest To God* as "the most consistent statement I know" of "... the only ethic for 'man come of age' " (pp. 116f.; Robinson was referring specifically to Fletcher's article in the *Harvard Divinity Bulletin* for October 1959, "The New Look in Christian Ethics"). In his book Fletcher spells out his conviction that Christian love, *agape,* must be the basis of ethics for Christians. Love in action solves everything.

Fletcher excels in vigor and forthright statement, which is one of the reasons why his book is an excellent one to read in order to seize the atmosphere as well as the detail of the New Morality. He is nothing if not convinced that the type of ethic he espouses is unconditionally right and unconditionally Christian. "In its very marrow," he writes, "Christian ethics is a situation ethic" (p. 77). His enthusiasm for his position is boundless and bold. He interlaces his theory with an abundance of illustration and anecdote. The reader who is hurried along the road of his New Morality may perhaps wish that Fletcher had separated the various strands of his argument to permit a more leisurely scrutiny of the various parts of his "nonsystem," as he calls it. But, at any rate, there is no obscurantism or mystification or ambiguous phrasing here. The author has said plainly the things he wants to say, and said them with a directness that leaves no room for major misunderstanding of his meaning.

Whether the things he has said clarify or obscure the subject he is discussing is another matter. The dust jacket of *Situation Ethics* carries the statement, "Situationism is the crystal precipitated in Christian ethics by our era's pragmatism and relativism." It goes on to observe,

> This candid and passionate brief for individual responsibility is completely attuned to our secular society — and to existential modern man, who has learned with the atom bomb that existence not only demands decision, but *is* decision.

If we do not happen to be convinced that modern pragmatism and relativism and secularity can penetrate to "the very marrow" of the Christian ethic, and if we do not share the view of existential modern man that existence is decision (a conclusion, incidentally, the existentialists learned to accept long before the atom bomb), we may not be altogether reassured that the light has finally shone to banish the darkness in which the topic of Christian behavior has hitherto been plunged. There is a lack of clarity, to begin with, about the very name of situation ethics that should make us pause before joining in the loud hallelujahs that have greeted the precipitation of this particular crystal in the solution of our contemporary ideologies.

The dictionary definition of the word "ethics" is "science of morality." Ethical "science" or theory supplies us with principles that can be used to guide us in the performance of individual moral acts, much in the same way that the science of architecture guides us in constructing individual architectural buildings. Now, when we act, we act in particular situations; just as, when we build, we build on particular sites. To speak of a situation ethic, then, is rather like speaking about site architecture. Obviously, no building can be designed without being conditioned by the site; and no *good* building can be expected to arise unless the building is adapted to the site both structurally and aesthetically. Yet no one would ever imagine that just knowing all about the site would enable us to build anything on it, minus the knowledge of architectural principles. Similarly, knowing all about a situation in which moral action is to be carried out cannot, by itself, guide us to ethical action. Without principles, there is no way of acting ethically in any situation. The name "situation ethics," as a description of an ethical theory, makes no sense, unless you have a philosophy repudiating the traditional approach to ethics.

However, Fletcher did not invent the name but found it ready to hand. And he is anxious to dissociate the name from the "existentialist" ethic with which it has been linked, an ethic that does deny principles. He himself is all for principles, he explains, though not for rules. He insists that "situationism is a *method,* not a substantive ethic" (p. 34; italics his).

This being explained, we may wonder why Fletcher has confused his readers by calling his book *Situation Ethics.* Had he called it *Situational Method in Ethics* we should have known what he was doing there. Apparently this is not what Robinson thought he was doing, namely, giving us the only ethic for man-come-of-age. Or is it? Fletcher often uses the word "strategy" in *Situation Ethics,* and a treatise on ethical strategy for Christians would have been highly useful. But it would not have posed as a New Morality. It would not have laid down the principles that Fletcher has strewn all through his book; since strategy is carrying out principles, not determining what they are. And it would not have mounted the judge's bench reserved for "substantive" ethics, and declared (in a chapter heading) that ethical law says "Love Only Is Always Good." For, make no mistake about it, *Situation Ethics* assumes that it has a specific ethical theory to present, which is an unconditional Love Ethic. The strategy is unconditional. It "is the strategy of love" (p. 31).

Most often when a thinker says he is not giving a system, what we discover is that he is not setting out his system in an orderly manner, but giving it all jumbled up, leaving his readers to sort it out for themselves. But this by no means indicates that his system is flexible, for in fact it may prove to be a system of the most rigid kind that he is asking us to accept. Fletcher's "nonsystem" emerges as one oddly at variance with the pragmatic and relativistic approach that he says he is taking to the subject. At every turn — though not in an orderly sequence — we are told exactly what each of the leading terms of ethics (justice, value, goodness, conscience, means and ends, etc.) *is* and *is not;* why the traditional ethical systems fall short of the truth of situation ethics; where the great theologians of the past and present are to be commended when they seem to come near being situationists, and are to be blamed (or commiserated with) when they finally fail to see the light; and how we can know what Christianity is and recognize the Holy Spirit.

Fletcher's contention that the situationist *method* solves, in principle, all our ethical problems is reminiscent of the claims of the supporters of homeopathic medicine that this method solves all the problems of health. Of course, a method that is supposed to be universally efficacious presupposes a knowledge of the whole reality of the sphere (ethics or medicine) in which the method is to be employed. It tacitly assumes an omniscience in this sphere, which is able to reject dogmatically every alternative approach to the subject. Its confidence in being *the* approach is consequently unbounded, and it has no patience with the "yes but ..." and the "maybe, yet on the other hand ..." that would suggest that one single comprehensive system may not be able to do justice to all the complexities of existence. The first question that both Fletcher's conclusions and his tone of arguing raise is whether his method is the one and only sufficient method. The second question, probing deeper, is whether his view of the whole subject of Christian ethics is tenable at all, or whether a too simple posing of the problem to be faced has resulted in an overconfident solution that actually avoids dealing with the problem at all.

On the first question, my own reaction would be to say that Fletcher's situationist method provides a wholly proper strategy to employ in one area of ethical concern, namely, in person-to-person dealings. Here the strategy of love (in the sense of goodwill and concern for the value of the other as a person) must prevail. In this area rules do not apply, and principles have to be used simply as guidelines to allow us to assess how

114

we are to treat the unique situation. This is analogous to the problem confronting the architect whenever he plans to erect a building on a particular site. The architect cannot say, "The Parthenon is the perfect building, therefore I will erect a replica of the Parthenon." He has to ask himself what the building is needed for, and how best he can locate a suitable building on this particular site, meeting the special requirements of the job (cost, material, labor, etc.). The result will be only one possible solution of the problem, will be only approximately successful, and — perhaps most important of all — will help him to be a better architect in the future only to the extent to which it teaches him to distrust all general rules and have complete respect for the unrepeatable elements in each building situation. Nevertheless, his ability to react imaginatively and inventively to the unique situation does not in itself make him a good architect. He must also have expert knowledge of the rules of construction, and of the laws governing these rules (strength of materials, etc.), or his building will simply fall down.

So, too, in ethics concern for persons, goodwill, and freedom from preconceived notions of how to handle individual situations is not enough. It is *a* strategy. It is one element in ethical behavior. It does not follow, to begin with, that loving concern is what ought to guide us in handling groups where persons are not met individually, and where justice is the end we have to pursue. To think the strategy of love applies here will soon lead us into absurdity — and into immoral behavior.

Fletcher says dogmatically:

> Justice is nothing other than love working out its problems. This viewpoint has existed potentially for a long time. Now we state it flatly and starkly so that there is no mistaking what is said. Love=justice; justice=love (p. 95).

To say this "flatly and starkly" does not suffice, however, to make it true. Fletcher's argument is that justice is love calculating in terms of prudence, involving *"a loving use of force"* (p. 100; italics his). President Truman's decision to drop the atomic bomb on Hiroshima and Nagasaki, for example, was made on "a vast scale of 'agapeic calculus'" (p. 98). This is surely the *reductio ad absurdum* of the Love Ethic. It involves an entire disregard of the reason why political choices are made, and of the ends sought by political action. It assumes that President Truman might conceivably have broadcast to Japan the message, "Sorry to have to annihilate you folks, but it's a choice of love!"—which would either have been the statement of a lunatic suffering from a messianic delusion, or an expression of the most immoral cynicism. The end result of trying to put love into politics is graphically illustrated in the ending of George Orwell's novel *1984*. There the hero, having betrayed the girl who has been his partner not only in love but also in his struggle against the injustice of the totalitarian State, sits, a moral wreck, imagining that he *loves* Big Brother, the symbol of the State ruling through the Ministry of Love (Secret Police).

The statesman possessing moral probity knows that in doing his duty he *ought not* to be concerned with love, however much he may "love" his people. His concern is for their corporate well-being. His work is first to preserve the State, and second to direct its power in the interests of justice. That is why there may be real — and tragic — conflicts between the public and the private conscience. It was the prudence of statesmanship that crucified Jesus, conceiving the welfare of a whole people more important than a single life (John 11:50). At least, Caiaphas seems not to have imagined he was really choosing on the scale of "agapeic calculus." Fletcher could have supplied him with a full justification for his action, even had he overheard the teaching of Jesus about loving our enemies, and wondered whether he ought not to forgive this man, his enemy because he was a threat to the well-being of the people. The situation calculus runs: "It is right to deal lovingly with the enemy *unless to do so hurts too many friends*" (p. 115; italics his). Yet it is unlikely that Caiaphas, or anyone else called to exercise political power, would be able to accept the situationist translation of public duty into terms applicable only to private morality.

The outcome of trying to produce a single maxim embracing both justice and love, indeed, is that the result fits neither sphere. Loving our enemies so long as our friends are not hurt too extensively is a principle that would hardly satisfy a St. Francis of Assisi on the one hand, or a Machiavelli on the other. Its formula for combining love and self-interest succeeds only in advising us to have the innocence of serpents and the wisdom of doves.

116

At the beginning of the present chapter I spoke about the way in which religion is concerned with reliable standards of conduct rooted in the will of God, and thus stands in tension with all humanistic ethics that seek to explore the nature of the good "for its own sake," where the chief assumption is that, for good to be really good, it must advance the well-being of man.

Fletcher adopts the relativistic, pragmatic, and utilitarian approach to ethics characteristic of modern non-Christian ethical systems. Indeed, by explicitly choosing to stress a utilitarianism (the theory that the good is the greatest happiness of the greatest number) of a rigid nineteenth-century type rather than any of the ethical systems postulating a notion of "intrinsic" values, he has adopted an ethic radically at odds with Christian belief. At the same time, he is determined to lay down a single, absolute good. He insists that in all dimensions of human life there is only one thing needful — to love our neighbor. This is God's will for man, his declared intention communicated through Christ.

As a result, there is a remarkable division in Fletcher's thinking. He starts out by seeking the good for man, and finds that it is man's freedom to seek his own good (the happiness of the majority) without reference to anything outside the world of man. And yet he retains the wholly religious concern for one absolute standard.

It appears that, like the secularist Christians, Fletcher wants religion, and wants it secular. He says that there are no religiously sanctioned laws any more; nothing is either good or bad in itself; and we are fully free to decide for ourselves how we are to behave in any situation. And then he turns around and insists that there is, nevertheless, one changeless law, the law of love which is always binding in each and every situation. We have to obey this law "religiously," so to speak. Yet we are still completely free to decide how we are to behave, because we must decide for ourselves, in each and every instance, what is the loving thing to do. And what we conscientiously decide will be loving, even if it seems hateful and gives other people hell.

Fletcher's motive throughout is to fight legalism in Christian conduct, and a petrified authoritarianism in Christian life generally. The revealed will of God being the final standard for the Christian, the Bible and/or the Church have been tradition-

117

ally the final authority for the way to live the Christian life. And Christians have been all too prone to forget how easily divine law, when humanly interpreted, can degenerate into "the tradition of men" (Mark 7:8). They have found it easier to take the answers mechanically and legalistically, especially concentrating on the "sins" to be avoided (at least publicly), and finding all too little place for Jesus' words about the single eye (Luke 11:34-36) and the evil that comes out of the heart (Mark 7:18-23).

It is against this desire for easy, ready-made solutions to ethical problems that Fletcher and other situationists in large measure fight — not just the desire to have available religious standards, but to have these standards fixed beyond the complexity of real existence and its ambiguous events. The battle cannot be said not to be worth fighting still in the Christian camps, both Catholic and Protestant. Protestantism has much constructive work to show on the subject, some of it going far back in Protestant history. Protestant practice is something else again, for where it has recoiled from religious hypermoralism it has most often lapsed into religious indifferentism. Rome's recent reform has meant a revolution in theory, so that some Roman Catholic moral theologians have become ardent situationists. A sudden change from an authoritarian ethical climate was bound to lead to that kind of development. Meanwhile, the practical effect is startling, though predictable. When such a nonmoral rule of conduct as eating fish on Fridays is withdrawn, no great intelligence is required to see that soon sections of the laity will be found demanding that the Pope reopen such a serious moral issue as birth control — and even tell him the way it ought to be settled.

The situationists, all the same, may be fighting the battle on the wrong front; or, to change the metaphor, they may be treating a disease by a drug that induces a far more deadly disease in the patient. The problems lies, as I have indicated, not in situationism as a strategy, but in asserting that it is the only strategy because it is an ethical absolute.

For Christians love *is* an absolute. That we should love one another is the "new commandment" (John 15:12) of the Lord of Christians, and thus an absolute command. But what situationists overlook is that the Christian calling to stand in the obedience of love is not an ethical standard, for it is grounded in faith in the God who is love and in the Son through whom the Father's love was declared to the world. Certainly it has ethical implications, and direct ones. The Christian does not love "as I have loved you" by merely remembering his brother lovingly while he is in church, or reading the Bible, or saying his prayers. The place for demonstrating brotherly love is "in the world" and in day-to-day relations. But Christian love is not a simple possibility in the world, since the world does not acknowledge God (Rom. 1:28-32) and did not either know or receive his Son (John 1:10-11). Man, not excluding Christian man, is a sinner; and his sinfulness enters into each and every situation where he meets his brother.

The Christian situationist, like the secular Christian, holds lightly what Anselm called "the heavy weight" of sin. Both Robinson (*Honest To God*, p. 119) and Fletcher (p. 79) fuss over translating Augustine's *dilige et quod vis fac* "Love with care, and *then* what you will do," rather than "Love and do as you like." Personally, I think Augustine's meaning comes over just as well in idiomatic English as in pedantic paraphrase; but, if there is fuss to be made, I would make it over the fact that the Doctor of Grace is referring to the life lived in grace and forgiveness, to Christian love and not to any love trying to be situationally prudent. He is speaking about those who are citizens of the Heavenly City built on love of God, and who live beside, yet are separated from, the citizens of the Earthly City built on love of self. Every estimate the Christian makes of the world around him must take into account that ours is a fallen world, simultaneously under the wrath and the mercy of God. To attempt to think of the world as a single world, seeking one end, manifesting one love, and lacking only the perfection that resolute and responsible action will ultimately achieve for it, is to lose all contact with historic Christian faith. It is also, incidentally, to fail to appreciate the rich diversity of the relative values displayed in God's marvelously intricate creation, by trying to absolutize them.

Just as the champion of secular Christianity is not content to let the world be the world of both secular and religious values but insists upon treating it religiously as though it were the Kingdom of God, so the Christian situationist is not content to

119

let human conduct pursue both human and divine ends but insists upon estimating it religiously under the absolute of love. Although Fletcher insists that the strategy of love meets each situation without rules, in point of fact behind each of his examples of situationist solutions to moral problems lies an undeclared universal rule governing that particular situation. Occasionally these rules come unexpectedly to the surface. Thus, when discussing a problem of abortion, Fletcher writes of the situationists' probable decision: "It is even likely they would favor abortion for the sake of the victim's self-respect or reputation or happiness or simply on the ground that *no unwanted and unintended baby* should ever be born" (p. 39; italics his). Here the "no . . . ever . . ." cannot be other than a universal rule.

Yet this rule is a peculiar one in being both universal and also no more than "likely." The reason for this is that the absoluteness of a religious standard is combined with the relativity of a secular-utilitarian calculation of the "greatest good." This is the same phenomenon of investing a piece of this world with a transcendent quality that has been pointed out in connection with secular Christianity. The rule governing any situation is only likely — because we ourselves, human beings with a human perspective, have to lay it down. Yet, once made, it has the binding force of a divine command. The voice of the people, for situation ethics, is indeed the voice of God. As Israel believed that God said, "Thou shalt not commit adultery," so the situationist Christian believes that man is now saying, "Thou shalt have no unwanted and unintended baby." Both commands, as commands, have equal force; only man is unlike God in that he not only can change but is always changing. This is why the situation is all-important (since man's latest pronouncement is the sole binding one), and this is why Fletcher insists that situationism is concerned with "antecedent rather than consequent judgment" (p. 54), that is, makes decisions but does not judge them afterwards (since man's decisions will change again next time, there is no point in saying they were either right or wrong last time).

That man speaks with God's authority and like God himself, is axiomatic for Fletcher. He describes the Christian situationist saying to his neighbor, a non-Christian situationist,

Your love is like mine, like everybody's; it is the Holy Spirit.

> Love is not the work of the Holy Spirit, it *is* the Holy Spirit —
> working in us . . . (p. 54; italics his).

On this reckoning the Holy Spirit is the spirit of man when he is morally concerned, and so open to love. The Holy Spirit for Paul is the one who floods the hearts of believers with the love of God (Rom. 5:5) ; and for John he is the one who proves that those who confess Christ dwell in God and he in them (1 John 4:13). But the situationist is sure that our consciousness of personal involvement in human situations *is* the Holy Spirit. Human love is divine, and its decision the will of the Holy Spirit.

The situationist feels that the Holy Spirit works by directing him to work towards "secular" ends (psychic freedom, reputation, family happiness, health, virility, self-affirmation, and so on). Augustine, however, places another valuation upon the view that seeks "all its good here upon earth." In *The City of God* he writes of earthly peace and its concomitant blessings:

> Doubtless those results are good and God's good gifts. But if the things appertaining to that celestial and supernal city where the victory shall be everlasting, be neglected for those goods, and those goods desired as the only goods, or loved as if they were better than the others, misery needs must follow and increase that which is inherent before (xv. 4).

Here it is assumed that everybody's love is very far from being the same.

Augustine is a supreme ethical realist, and his warning that our attempts to decrease misery often lead to its increase is worth noting. Fletcher, by way of contrast, is completely contemptuous in his reference to those who would maintain a literal "fall" of man, or suggest that the call to live by love alone must fail because of human egocentricity. The slogan of Christian situationism might well be, he says, Paul's words (Gal. 5:1), "For freedom Christ has set us free; stand therefore and do not submit again to a yoke of slavery" (p. 81). After italicizing the word "has" and explaining that "a yoke of slavery" means "law," he does not trouble to explain that he has "secularized" St. Paul's words. Nor does he explain that he is assuming we now live in the Kingdom of Heaven, where Christ rules in final triumph over "captive death and conquered sin"— or rather, will do so when man by his loving works has achieved this end. Once again, we see how the world-view that elevates the secular sphere to a religious ultimate assumes religion to be a matter of good works that man may easily do if he puts his mind to it, and must do if he is not to be left behind by the inevitable advance of human progress. Fletcher even makes the "obligation" to love (note how love now becomes transformed into a law) a command written into the constitution of the universe. God's grace is turned into a universal law. He writes:

> People are, in any case, going to have to grow up into situation ethics, no doubt of it. The Christian is called to be mature, to live by grace and freedom, to *respond* to life, to be responsible. This is the vocation of all situationists, most certainly the "calling" of Christian situationists (p. 82).

Christian or non-Christian, we are equally to respond to life, as the equivalent to the call to respond to Christ. The New Testament tells us that we leave behind the childish state when we grow up into Christ (Eph. 4:13-15). But Fletcher tells us that what we must grow up into is situation ethics. Now we know what we are to worship, and where we are to find truth. Could idolatry be taken further?

One of the most telling of modern parables is William Golding's *Lord of the Flies,* in which human society is pictured as a company of small boys left alone on a Pacific island after the crash of their plane has killed the pilot. As they set up a rudimentary organization for their society, the most prudent (to use Fletcher's term) of the boys remarks that they must hang on to "the rules," for "the rules are the only thing we've got." And so it proves, when civil war soon breaks out among them. The miniature society is saved from total destruction only by the fortuitous arrival of a naval boat, bringing adult "law" to put an end to the slaughter.

Because Fletcher generally takes for his examples small-scale situations, securely set within a reign of law, he has no difficulty in showing that cutting across accepted moral standards for the sake of "love" is frequently the way to obtain immediate "happiness." He can as easily show that the law in its detailed operation is often, as Charles Dickens' Mr. Bumble commented, an ass that needs guiding by enlightened common sense. When he casts his eyes on a wider situation, for example the decision to use the atomic bomb, his trust in human ability benevolently to use the "agapeic calculus" appears incredibly naive. Love is the fulfilling of the law (Rom. 13:10), but only perfect beings could ever work at fulfilling the law — as situationism demands — by willing to love. Since we do not live in the Kingdom of Heaven, the law, imperfectly reflected in human "rules," is God's indispensable gift to sinful humanity, and "the only thing we've got" to stand between us and self-destruction. The shadow of the Bomb over our contemporary world should bring that home to us, Christian and non-Christian alike.

It is not enough for Fletcher to say, as he does (p. 85), that situationism is of course open to abuse and manipulation, but then so is every other ethical stance. The point is that some "strategies" are much more open than others, and that his formula of love as the only norm and the same as justice places no valid check upon human selfishness or cruelty. Deciding that we are to live without standards and behave in each situation as we see fit works splendidly, so long as we are a small minority in a law-abiding community; but the end of that road is anarchy and its twin, tyranny. Human law rightly regards the gravest threat to the rule of law to be contempt of law. If we are to adopt the view that there is nothing in itself good or bad, and that morality is finding means to serve ends, and that the end of all ends is love, we will soon find ourselves looking into the eyes, not of Christ or of our situationist neighbor, but of Big Brother.

Love is the law of the Kingdom of Heaven. But love that is made into a law for the City of Man is not simply un-Christian. It is also inhuman.

Part 5

HOW TO REGRESS BY WANTING ONLY TO PROGRESS, AND HOW TO BE CONTEMPORARY BY NOT BEING AFRAID OF THE PAST

ELEVEN

THE RETURN OF LIBERALISM

Look, where it comes again!
— *William Shakespeare,* Hamlet

In "The Debate Continues," John Robinson's summing up at the end of *The Honest To God Debate,* there is an interesting footnote. Robinson has been speaking of Paul van Buren's attempt in *The Secular Meaning of the Gospel* to combine the insights of linguistic philosophy with "an orthodox Christology based on Barth and Bonhoeffer." His footnote (note 3, p. 250) adds the comment that this "shows, incidentally, how facile it is to see current theological radicalism, as some have, simply as a new version of liberal modernism," whereas it actually cuts across the accepted theological and ecclesiastical lines.

Maybe Robinson's dismissal of the reading of the shape of current radicalism in theology as a return to liberal modernism is itself a little too facile. In an article entitled "Theology in the Context of Culture" (originally written for the *Christian Century* series "How I Am Making Up My Mind" and now published in *Frontline Theology*), van Buren himself has written that his book was a step in overcoming his theological past and "served to help me over a hump" (p. 48). He tells in the same article how he had been educated to believe that nineteenth-century developments in religious thinking were a dead end, afterwards corrected in "neo-classic" and "biblical" theology. Now he thinks these later developments were a temporary diversion trying to go back to a past that is gone for ever, and that we have the task of going back and taking up again where the nineteenth century left off. For there was then a genuine at-

127

tempt to find a contemporary form of religion; and we must not bother about the traditional pattern of the Judeo-Christian faith, but find how that pattern can be "developed, interpreted, or adapted" to serve contemporary needs.

So it seems that van Buren's concern with an orthodox Christology, together with Barth and Bonhoeffer as proponents of the traditional Judeo-Christian tradition, was for him a temporary phase to be put resolutely behind him. The liberal-modernist line in nineteenth-century religious thought turns out to be the one he wishes to pursue.

The nineteenth century, as I have already indicated in connection with van Buren and in various other places, keeps turning up wherever one looks carefully at the New Theology. Not the least of the echoes of nineteenth-century ways of thinking is John Robinson's *Honest To God* itself.

Though completely forgotten now, a book by a British writer about the necessity for breaking through to a new form of Christianity both intellectually and morally adapted to the needs of modern men appeared in 1888, and made an immediate and sensational impression on both sides of the Atlantic. Like so many of the social and religious tracts for the times in those days, it was a novel. *Robert Elsmere* was by Mrs. Humphrey Ward, née Mary Arnold, a niece of the Matthew Arnold whose *St. Paul and Protestantism* (1870), *Literature and Dogma* (1873), and *God and the Bible* (1875) had proposed a demythologizing of Scripture long before the advent of Rudolf Bultmann. The hero of the novel was a young Anglican priest whose own "reluctant revolution" finally carried him outside the Church to prove the truth of Christianity separated from its "envelope of miracle" and concentrated upon an affirmation of the present power of Jesus, by a life of service for others. Robert Elsmere found himself compelled to move "beyond theism," and also to refuse, on his deathbed, to admit a supernatural Christ who atoned for our sins. His inspiration was one of his teachers at Oxford, a philosopher named Grey, whose radicalism both in matters of belief and social action he had earlier rejected but finally found, through his parish experience, to be the only relevant gospel for modern man. The figure of Grey was, in fact, a close portrait of the English Hegelian T. H. Green, Professor of Moral Philosophy at Oxford. Green taught, as Tillich was to do later, that

God must not be thought to be *a* Being, since he is the supreme reality in which the spiritual life of man participates, and that Christianity essentially proclaims this truth.

The parallel between *Robert Elsmere* and *Honest To God* is almost uncanny, extending as it does even to verbal similarities and to the unexpectedly wide welcome both works received. At least, it would be uncanny, were the former not so clearly an earlier version, in fictional form, of the latter. The question that is intriguing is why the newness of the New Theology is so widely urged to be proof of its claim to represent the way forward for contemporary man. There is very little being said by the Christian radicals today that, allowing for differences in expression, would have sounded fresh to the good Victorians who read *Robert Elsmere*. Our current slogans and catchwords were not around then, but the ideas they stand for were already being circulated widely. The change in the moral climate today undoubtedly would have made them rub their eyes, although they understood quite well that changes in belief always demand changes in moral standards. Through most of the nineteenth century the Victorian middle-class ethic was still so strong that Matthew Arnold, who considered it his special mission to attack it in its stronghold of "the Nonconformist conscience," seemed to make little headway. Nevertheless, only a few years after Arnold's death George Bernard Shaw was propounding the theories that have been taken up by the present-day champions of the New Morality; and the public, after the initial shock, was largely delighted.

Of course, it may still be argued that the way spelled out in *Robert Elsmere* (and in the general line of thinking that inspired it) *is* the one way ahead for contemporary man. Yet a confident claim to be breaking new ground, when you are in fact threshing old straw, does little to increase other people's confidence in your reliability, especially if you are insisting that your watchword is honesty. To be either ignorant of, or indifferent to, the pedigree of your ideas is not a good recommendation to give in support of your ability to understand fully what you are saying when you expound these ideas.

So Robinson, for instance, would have strengthened his case considerably, as well as removing all kinds of misunderstanding, had he said that he believed that the tradition of nineteenth-

129

century philosophical idealism, stemming from Hegel and finding a forceful contemporary supporter in Tillich, was the best
foundation for a Christian view of God in the world today. As it
is, he leaves us all to imagine that the notion of God as ultimate
reality and not a supernatural Person is a wholly new idea that
has arisen in these last days of twentieth-century enlightenment.
When we discover for ourselves that this new way of picturing
God is actually a very ancient one — since it certainly did not
arise first in the nineteenth century, although its Hegelian form
happens to be the one in which it has come down to us today —
we are likely to question whether it is so obviously relevant to our
modern way of thinking after all.

Similarly, when Robinson called us to consider Bonhoeffer's
notion of a religionless Christianity, he might have mentioned
that "religion" for Bonhoeffer was construed after the meaning
he had learned from Karl Barth, where religion represents man's
attempt to find his own God and is contrasted with revelation,
or God's way of making himself known to us in Jesus Christ. He
might also have pointed out that this particular understanding of
"religion" has no connection whatsoever with the idealistic understanding of the word, according to which (as in Tillich's
usage) religion means the awareness of ultimate reality that man
has in the depths of his spirit. For Bonhoeffer religion is idolatry,
and living under the authority of the Christian revelation is
alone the life of genuine faith. For Tillich any exclusive attach-
ment to one revelation is idolatry, and faith is *a hidden power
within ourselves,* to utilize which is true religion. Thus the one
asserts what the other denies. An idealistic philosophy of religion distrusts religions, but believes in the pure essence of
religion manifest partially in them all. Faith in the Christian
revelation rejects all religions — including the Christian religion
insofar as it models itself on the pattern of other religions —
believing that the Christian gospel does not teach faith in a
God we can find within ourselves or in our own depths, but
instead tells us about the God who makes himself available to
us in Jesus Christ, the Crucified.

When in *Letters and Papers from Prison* Bonhoeffer speaks
of liberal theology, he characterizes it as "abridging the gospel"
(p. 167) and going off "into the typical liberal reduction process
(the 'mythological' elements of Christianity are dropped, and

130

Christianity is reduced to its 'essence')" (p. 199). The abridg-
ment of the gospel that Bonhoeffer speaks of is necessarily a dis-
counting of the particular events upon which the New Testament message is based, reducing these events to the status of
stories (myths) illustrating some general truth about the nature
of the universe. Such a "reduction process" turns the God of
biblical revelation into a symbol of the divinity we are aware
of within ourselves. Because the God-in-the-depths is the hypothesis required for a particular world-view (in Tillich's case,
the Absolute of idealistic philosophy), liberal reductionism
leaves us with a some*thing*, never a Being, a Some One. When
Robinson expresses his understanding of the articles of Christian
belief, as he does in *But That I Can't Believe,* he comes down
to a "typical" liberal reduction in most instances. He declares his
faith in an *it* manifest partially in all religions. His essay "Do
We Need a God?" talks much about the need for encountering
a *Thou* in life, but ends in a series of affirmations about an
it or "level of reality." He writes that the universe discloses itself
at different levels, yet

> The level of reality for which men have required the word
> "God" is one that presupposes and underlies all these others. It is
> evidenced in the response to the sacred. . . . It comes in many
> forms. . . . This is the reality which the believer finds it impossible
> to deny. . . . He may not represent it as "a" Person — though the
> nearest analogy in his experience is the kind of claim that needs
> him in personal relationships. But, however dimly perceived
> or obeyed, it is for him, as supremely it was for Jesus, the
> reality in whose grace and power the whole of his life is lived
> (p. 61).

A level of reality cannot really be a *Thou.* It seems we call
God *a* Being simply because the highest values written into
the universe are personal for us, and so by an inadequate yet
necessary analogy we personify the ultimate level, the final *it*.
When we speak of it as showing "grace," again we are merely
speaking metaphorically. This understanding of Robinson's intention seems to be confirmed when we see him speaking as
liberals, especially liberals of the school of Ritschl, used to speak
about Jesus living his life in the realization of the power of
this level of reality. Ritschlian liberals were convinced that
what we should discover to be true Christianity was not faith

in Jesus but sharing the faith *of* Jesus in God's power to bring his Kingdom through dedicated humanity. We may feel that our understanding of Robinson along these lines is correct when we find him stating, in his essay on "The Holy Spirit," that the holy Spirit of God is embodied though not confined to the Church, where it is seen as the Spirit of Christ in the fellowship of the Church. He adds, "This is where men should be able to recognize the Spirit for what it most truly is" (p. 85). The Spirit appears to be another *it,* manifest in human fellowship.

In spite of his denial that the New Theology is a return to liberal modernism, Robinson in these and other places seems to be following the liberal modernist line without question or hesitation. Yet we would be wrong to imagine that such is his conscious intention. There are other places — for example, his final essay "In Sum" (pp. 122-127) — where he says he rejects the liberal faith in the faith of Jesus, affirming his belief in the primacy of the Lordship of Jesus and the centrality of the cross. Here he explains that his main concern is a missionary one, that he begins at the place where people are in order to bring them to see for themselves what Christianity is all about. Today in our approach to leading men to Christianity, "the way through is *from* experience *to* authority, from relationships to revelation, from immanence to transcendence, rather than the other way round" (p. 124; italics his).

If this is truly Robinson's strategy, as he declares it to be, we may wonder why he himself so often makes theological statements that, in authentic liberal fashion, stop at experience, relationships, and immanence without ever proceeding to authority, revelation and (more than that which Bonhoeffer calls "epistemological") transcendence. This would surely not have happened had he been critically alert to the tradition of Christian thinking out of which he wished to argue the case for Christianity. Lack of clear thinking on this point means that he perpetually halts between two opinions, one moment adopting a liberal-modernist stance, and another moment speaking from the perspective of a Christianity based on the historic creeds.

Robinson fixes his gaze so much upon where he would like to be — at the place where Christian faith becomes acceptable to the world's way of thinking — that he does not notice he has shifted his starting point in order to accommodate the world.

And he strives to convince the unbelieving world that it is much more Christian than it thinks. What it rejects is not essential to the Christian faith. What it accepts is, implicitly though not explicitly, Christian. Because of this ambiguity in his own outlook, it is difficult to take his proposed missionary strategy altogether seriously. One can hardly plan the best route to his destination unless he knows where he is when he starts.

It was the liberalism of Tillich, Bonhoeffer reminds us, that made him wish to show that the religious thinker understood the world better than the world understood itself. The last public lecture Tillich gave was one entitled "The Significance of the History of Religions for the Systematic Theologian" (*The Future of Religions,* 1966, pp. 80-94). In it he strongly rejected "the paradox of a religion of non-religion, or a theology without theos, also called a theology of the secular" (p. 80). Tillich saw very clearly the fact that I have been referring to throughout, namely, that secular Christianity can mean nothing else except a religious valuation of the secular, an attempt to identify God with the City of Man. Tillich naturally denounced this attempt, because it denied the central affirmation of his religious philosophy by making the finite process of human history divine; whereas Tillich's concept of divinity was one making God the transcendent Ground of all being, a reality manifest in everything, and contained in nothing. Yet the conflict here, where Tillich takes issue with the religion of secularism, is, in the end, simply a quarrel between two types of liberalism.

Both "theologies" take God's transcendence to be what Bonhoeffer calls "a partial extension of the world." For Tillich this extension is always "in the depths" of the world, and is never to be identified with any one aspect of the world exclusively. For the Christian secularists this extension is found when man immerses himself wholly in the world and finds a power working there that beckons him on to a future when God will finally reveal himself. In other words, Tillich remains faithful to classical philosophy, which keeps to the static picture of the world found in Greek thought, where reality is always present as a hidden Ground of everything that appears. The Christian secularist, on the other hand, favors a dynamic picture of the world, where God is the hidden power working within world history. He is no motionless Being-itself, but a process ever changing with the advance of human consciousness and human achievement. But these two contrasting pictures of the world produce alike a version of Christianity that carries out Bonhoeffer's description of liberal theology. Liberal theology, says Bonhoeffer, "allowed the world the right to assign Christ his place in the world" (*Letters and Papers*, p. 197). So for Tillich Christ's function is to reveal, at one point in the world, the hidden Ground of being. For the Christian secularist Christ's function is to reveal a decisive point in the world's history, at which the hidden divine power working in history brings to man a new consciousness of his freedom and responsibility to create the City of Man as a place of human values.

I have concentrated once again in the present chapter on Robinson, because, as I argued earlier, *Honest To God* is an excellent representative example of the New Theology, in that it picks up so many of the tendencies floating around in today's air and tries to combine them all. Thus it shows more of what is going on in the way of current religious thinking than more obviously radical theologies that pursue one line right to its logical or illogical end. Robinson's belief — expressed in *But That I Can't Believe* — that we ought to start "where people are," with *experience, relationships,* and *immanence,* is a good guide to other expressions of the New Theology in its patently liberal aspect of "abridging the gospel." Robinson's three terms are useful, for example, for examining the enthusiasm for "Christian secularity" that at the moment seems to have eclipsed other religious slogans in popularity.

A specifically philosophical version of secular Christianity has recently been produced by Schubert M. Ogden in *The Reality of God* (1966). Until a short time ago Ogden was fully in the Bultmannian camp, and he retains unaltered Bultmann's "liberal" belief that biblical myth must be removed before the "essence" of the gospel can stand forth. So Ogden simply assumes that the truth about God must be given in a philosophy. He still thinks Heidegger to be an important figure in the modern quest for an adequate philosophical God, but he now turns back for enlightenment more particularly to the process philosophies of Alfred North Whitehead and Charles Hartshorne. He finds in sight a New Theism. This will leave behind

134

such static concepts of the Absolute as Tillich's Being-itself, and will see God as "the unique or in all ways perfect instance of creative becoming," who "is related to the universe of other beings somewhat as the human self is related to its body" (p. 59), while being always perfect reality. This view of God will also establish, once and for all, the truth of secular Christianity; for, "rightly understood, Christianity has always been secular, because in its essence, in the presence in our human history of Jesus Christ, it is simply the representation to man and the world of their ultimate significance within the encompassing mystery of God's love" (p. 69).

Ogden's God-as-creative-becoming is an unambiguous philosophical Absolute. It is odd that Ogden withholds from it the name for which it so eminently qualifies, namely, Becoming-itself or the Ground of becoming. Although there are frequent references to the utter transcendence of this God, its transcendence is manifestly of the kind which Bonhoeffer called "an extension of the world," since its functions are to explain the presence of value in our world and also to guarantee the continuance of the world. This concept of God, incidentally, could well have been constructed (though it was not) around Robinson's three terms: (a) experience, (b) relationships, (c) immanence. Ogden affirms:

(a) New Theism is demanded because we must start to understand God out of our experience of ourselves (p. 57).

(b) God's perfection is measured in terms of relationships. While we are related to the rest of the universe only "in a radically inferior fashion," God is perfectly related to each and every part of it all the time. He is the "absolute ground of any and all real relationships" (p. 60).

(c) The end of God's perpetual becoming is to sanctify our secularity, assuring us of the "ultimate significance" of man and his world (p. 69). This is because "... the future for which we ultimately live our lives is neither merely our own nor that of others as limited as ourselves, but also the unending future of God's own creative becoming, in which we are each given to share" (p. 69).

Thus Christianity, reduced to its "essence" in classical liberal style, becomes the means of letting us know that, once beginning our quest for God out of our own experience, we do not after-

135

wards have to look beyond our existence for understanding the reality of God.

Ogden tells us that the theology he supports is postliberal, yet it looks like liberalism without any substantial alteration. Christ's coming is to inform us that our life has significance, and that "the radical claim of self-sacrificing love ... in Watts' words, demands our soul, our life, our all" (p. 204). "When I Survey the Wondrous Cross," after all, is about the unique significance of the cross of Christ, and of the unique demands Christ's love makes. Liberalism reduces this to a general principle of love that makes a universal demand upon us. We end, as Bonhoeffer commented in connection with Bultmann, with a universal truth.

Ogden's claim to have put secular Christianity on a firm basis seems slightly doubtful, since his philosophical theory requires us to posit an Absolute to guarantee the significance of our secular acts and decisions. Even though this view recognizes "our secular emphasis on man's full autonomy as a moral agent" (p. 69), it is asking rather much of secular man to keep speaking of God as the metaphysical glue that holds the secular universe together and cements values to facts. The secular Christianity of Harvey Cox is more consistent in that, although God is spoken of in his religious world-view, Cox admits that it may be best for secular man not to speak about God but rather to let him appear in his own good time.

Cox suggests, without meeting the question directly, that liberalism has no attractions for him. At least, he specifically disowns Tillich's metaphysical deity. He says, "Urban-secular man came to town after the funeral for the religious world-view was already over" (*The Secular City*, p. 70). And he praises Karl Barth for insisting on separating God and man in order to allow man freedom to live his own life (pp. 70-72).

Were we to judge by these few remarks where Cox puts down his religious roots, we might perhaps imagine him to be anti-liberal, cleaving to Barth's rejection of religion in the name of revelation, and therefore repudiating Tillich's notion of religion as the deep truth contained in human consciousness. We would then agree with William Hamilton's reference to Cox's work as "pop Barth." Yet that would be a great mistake.

If we look a little more closely, we will see that Cox's thinking moves entirely within the world bounded by the three terms

Robinson associates with current non-Christian consciousness.

(a) *Experience* is Cox's substitute for revelation. It is through examining the experience of the human race that he fixes his values, and in particular his valuation of biblical history. In his eyes the acts of God in history require no prophet to identify and interpret them. We can all see for ourselves how God is at work wherever human freedom is being advanced. Thus experience is self-validating. We know, for instance, that the social upheaval of our times is as far-reaching in its effects as the exodus was to Israel. Therefore, now as much as then, we must expect to learn a new name for God.

(b) *Relationships* on the human scale are so important for Cox that he wishes to model the modern Christian's attitude to God on the relationship of a grown son and a father doing a job together in partnership. On the basis of this analogy from human relationships, Cox concludes, "God wants man to be interested not in him but in his fellow man" (p. 232).

(c) *Immanence* is assumed in Cox's outlook. So when he talks about God being fully transcendent he says, "He meets us *in* the wholly other" (p. 229; italics added) — not, we should note, *as* the wholly other. The "wholly other" here seems to mean everything in the universe except man, that is, the conditions of nature. The thought that God might meet us otherwise than in some aspect of our experience of the created world never arises for Cox. Presumably, the only significance of Peter's confession that Jesus was the Christ, the Son of the living God (Matt. 16:17), was that Peter's experience of Jesus had convinced him Jesus had shown his disciples what responsible living in the world was like.

Cox's viewpoint corresponds quite exactly to "left-wing" Ritschlian liberalism, that type of liberalism believing that Jesus is the Christ because he sets us an example (rather than that he sets us an example because he is the Christ), and that the purpose of his coming was to show us how to build the Kingdom of God on earth. *The Secular City Debate* includes a discussion as to whether Cox has, or has not, simply reintroduced the Social Gospel, which was one of the products of left-wing Ritschlian theology. If we are to look for an anchorage of Cox's world-view and of his faith in the nonreligious religion of secular Christianity, I would suggest that, while Cox's thought owes something

137

to Ritschlian influences, its ultimate source is in the long-standing tradition in American Christianity that seeks, by one means or another, to locate the Kingdom of Heaven on earth.

Ernest B. Koenker's book *Secular Salvations* (1965) quotes on the first page a passage from Alex de Tocqueville's *Democracy in America* (1840) :

> The Americans not only follow their religion from interest, but they often place in this world the interest which makes them follow it. In the Middle Ages the clergy spoke of nothing but a future state; they hardly cared to prove that a sincere Christian may be a happy man here below. But the American preachers are constantly referring to the earth; and it is only with great difficulty that they can divert their attention from it. To touch their congregations, they always show them how favorable religious opinions are to freedom and public tranquility; and it is often difficult to ascertain from their discourses whether the principal object of religion is to procure eternal felicity in the other world or prosperity in this.

Cox's invitation to us to celebrate the liberties of the secular city and to accept its disciplines is, of course, much more than the latest republication of the theme of *The Kingdom of God in America* — to borrow the title of H. Richard Niebuhr's well-known book. Cox nowhere identifies the Kingdom of God with a particular form of political or social organization. Instead, he identifies it with the whole process of building the City of Man, of which "technopolis" is the stage we have reached at present.

What he has done is to adopt the *attitude* that de Tocqueville found in the America of his day, an attitude that played no small part in developing the secularist ideology of contemporary society. But his theoretical presuppositions are much more akin to those of the process philosophers than they are to a naive utopianism that would merge Christianity into the democratic principle. That is why, perhaps, he says in the "Afterword" to *The Secular City Debate* (pp. 197ff.) that he is now turning to Teilhard de Chardin and to Ernst Bloch for clarification of his ideas about God. Both these thinkers, the Christian evolutionist and the Marxist maverick, are process-minded. Back of their very different world-views lies the Hegelian vision of world history as the autobiography of Spirit. Almost any process thinker, indeed, could provide Cox with grist for his secular-religious mill. Before

1914 George Bernard Shaw had spoken, through the mouth of Lavinia in *Androcles and the Lion*, of the need to "strive for the coming of the God who is not yet." This is the idea of God that Cox thinks could open "an exciting new epoch in theology" ("Afterword," p. 202). New?!

What stares us in the face in *The Secular City* is that Cox's confidently stated theory that the metaphysical period of our history is over is strangely belied by his practice. As much as Ogden does, though without saying so, he assumes a metaphysical deity to explain why we can find full scope for our work of partnership with God in the service of technopolis. For this reason, Tillich's criticism of "the paradox of a religion of non-religion" is fully justified. It is only on the basis of "a religious world-view" that the City of Man could ever provide secular equivalents for religious values, enabling us to speak of a "theology of social change." Cox may think that he has put behind him the religious-metaphysical concept of a Ground of being; yet, if so, it is only to take up the alternative concept of a Ground of becoming.

In any case, liberalism furnishes the vision of the secular city. Bonhoeffer's characterization of liberalism as entailing a "typical reduction process" is illustrated in Cox's restatement of the Great Commandment of the gospel. Love to God is now declared to be reduced to love of man, since the revelation given in our experience of the historical process declares that God wants man to be interested not in him but in his fellow man. Similarly, the biblical gospel of salvation in Jesus Christ is demythologized and reduced to its "essence," which, the *Secular City* asks us to believe, is that man "must take responsibility in and for the city of man, or become once again a slave to dehumanizing powers" (p. 114). The religion of the secular demands self-salvation, self-prescribed.

TWELVE

LIBERAL AND CONSERVATIVE

I often think it's comical
How Nature always does contrive
That every boy and every gal
That's born into the world alive,
Is either a little Liberal,
Or else a little Conservative!
　　　　　　　— W. S. Gilbert, Iolanthe

If liberal theologies have produced so much confusion and so much distortion of historic Christianity, should we be safeguarding the future of the Christian faith in our day by placing ourselves firmly behind a conservative theology? Well, it would make life simpler if we could only file ourselves away about being in the right place. But life is more than one vast filing cabinet — although the way the secular city seems to be headed makes us wonder sometimes — and so we cannot solve all our problems by swearing to forsake liberalism for conservatism.

When Bonhoeffer pointed out that the weak point of liberal theology was that "it allowed the world the right to assign Christ his place in that world" (*Letters and Papers,* p. 197), he also said that its strong point was "that it did not seek to put back the clock." It is obviously wrong to change the way in which we interpret the gospel so drastically that we make it into another gospel. It is not necessarily right to think that the precise way the gospel was interpreted in the past is as necessary to preserve as the gospel itself. There are other means of preventing ourselves from throwing out the baby with the bath water than the one of never changing the water.

140

It would be pleasant if we could make a balanced theology by taking a little liberalism and a little conservatism (in the right proportions of course) and stirring well. But there is no easy "middle way" to be taken. For, just as faith is never found except clothed in the garment of one or other religious tradition, so liberal and conservative attitudes are not found unless clothed in the garment of a theological tradition (party, movement, school, etc.). There is no means of avoiding standing within a tradition. The more an individual consciously rejects the tradition in which he was reared, the more it is likely to influence him unconsciously. Yet one need not, for that reason, accept a tradition passively or uncritically. It is quite possible to adopt the outlook of a particular theological tradition and modify it through personal insights and perhaps also by learning from another tradition. This is what Bonhoeffer attempted to do when looking at the weaknesses and the strengths of liberal theology.

Bonhoeffer estimated liberalism directly in terms of the teaching of Karl Barth, from whom he had learned to oppose "religion" to "revelation." Barth, he said, "called the God of Jesus Christ into the lists against religion," by insisting upon the biblical distinction between "flesh" and "spirit" (p. 198). According to Barth the liberals had ignored the fact that the gospel is known because of God's revelation of himself in Christ, through his Holy Spirit, that is, by the action of "spirit" not "flesh." The liberals assumed that God's approach to us is through human consciousness, through our "spiritual" perception; and thus they confused "flesh" with "spirit." For Barth, therefore, to trust in the "flesh" and to trust in religion were one and the same. The Word of God is not the word of man, and does not become so when man appeals to his awareness of the spiritual depths in himself.

While starting from Barth's rejection of the liberal tradition, Bonhoeffer went on to criticize Barth for adopting what he called a "positivism of revelation," or what might be more popularly described as a take-it-or-leave-it attitude to the language of the Bible. The New Testament, Bonhoeffer believed, gives us the gospel story, a *true* story, and does not distort that story of God's dealing with men through the Incarnation in the interests of a world-view. Yet, on the other hand, the New Testament is written in the words of men who shared the

141

common world-view of their time. Their way of speaking about God and the world reflects the "religious" outlook of the first century (an outlook that New Testament scholars today try to reconstruct in order to advance our better understanding of the biblical record). So Bonhoeffer thought that Barth's positivism played into the hands of those who wanted a "conservative reconstruction," or standing rigidly on the words of the Bible as though the words were as authoritative as the message the words conveyed.

Bultmann saw rightly enough, so Bonhoeffer suggested, that our language and our thinking about the world today are not at all the same as that of the first century. But Bultmann wanted to alter the gospel story in order to make it fit neatly into the contemporary perspective. In other words, he wanted to make a twentieth-century "religion" normative for our understanding of biblical truth. Instead of freeing the New Testament message from its dated world-view, he had tried to impose upon that message another world-view that would soon be dated also. By considering that we can judge the credibility of the gospel story by asking what our modern scientifically-oriented culture thinks credible, he had missed the "real thing" and rejected biblical truth as being outdated myth. So, though wishing to improve upon Barth, Bultmann had actually relapsed into the old liberal error. He assumes that man knows within himself what the gospel *essentially* is all about. Therefore man today can separate this *essence* from the myths (primitive stories) of the biblical record, since the latter give us merely the essence glimpsed imperfectly in a time of much less enlightened knowledge (spirituality) than we now possess.

Bonhoeffer's rejection of Bultmann on the grounds that he had relapsed into liberalism shows us that he had no intention of going back behind Barth. Yet he also thought Bultmann's concern to avoid Barth's positivism was a necessary protest. Why he wished to avoid any "conservative restoration" was chiefly because conservatism tried to "put back the clock." We do not live in an age that can really be at home with the religious outlook of the first, or the fourth, or the fourteenth century. Furthermore, Bonhoeffer believed that the world had recently "come of age" and was learning that a religious outlook was not essential at all for understanding the world around us and man's day-to-day life in it.

I have argued (Chapter 8) that Bonhoeffer was overoptimistic in his estimate of the complete readiness of man-come-of-age for entering into a period of complete religionlessness. Be that as it may, his hope for finding a "worldly interpretation of Christianity" has been used to rehabilitate the very same liberal error that he fought against from first to last. However his thinking might have developed, there is no reason whatsoever for imagining that it would have departed from its basic conviction that religion is expendable because it is "flesh" claiming to be "spirit." A "liberal reconstruction" here is unthinkable.

New Theology has used Bonhoeffer's dissatisfaction with Barth's failure to help Christian *language* to adopt a twentieth-century idiom as an excuse to bring back the old liberal theology speaking in such an idiom. Entirely ignored in a theory of secular Christianity that fits Gogarten's theory of secularity well enough, but which is nearly always linked with the more highly regarded name of Bonhoeffer, is Bonhoeffer's belief that only the "imparted word of God" brings full freedom to the Christian for himself and towards his neighbor. The relative freedom that he envisaged as belonging to the natural world — and even then as existing only after Christ's forgiveness had been accepted — is turned into the dogma that all worldly freedom is God's work, which man must complete by taking up his own responsibility in and for the world.

New Theology has further assumed that to speak of man's coming of age is to indicate that man is freed *from God* rather than from religion (including liberal religion) and metaphysics or God-generating world-views; and that he is freed *for gaining his salvation through his good works* rather than for standing before God.

As we have seen, the explanations given by different spokesmen for the New Theology vary. Some (Robinson, Pike) say that God is to become fully believable by being no longer a supernatural Being; others (Christian atheists, New Christians) that we must will God's death and find God henceforth solely in man. A new metaphysics is hailed (by Ogden) to be the true metaphysics because it is not static; while the advent of

143

a world-view that has left behind a static Absolute is supposed (by Cox) to show that metaphysics is dead. No one has a good word to say for religion, and everyone speaks about the necessity for having an adequate, constructive, forward-looking, radical, twentieth-century theology; though there is a dearth of explanations as to why the word "theology" should be retained when the word "God" is either pronounced to be meaningless, almost meaningless, needing to be replaced, or descriptive of a dead entity belonging exclusively to a past era, and when it would seem that "religious philosophy" would be, in the circumstances, a wholly fitting title for any of the theories advocating a style of life fitted for "theologizing" without God or living in the secular waiting for a God that *is not* but *will be* when man has finished his work for him.

The plain truth of the matter seems to be that the New Theologies collectively — even in the mild, quasi-traditional form advanced by Robinson — all involve asserting either explicitly or implicitly that God is dead. The reason for this is that no "theology" (read "religious philosophy") can assert the full sufficiency of man to be responsible for the world and also find room for a *living* God. When once man asserts that the reality he knows lies in his own experience, his personal relationships, and his awareness of the immanence of a divine spirit in the depths of his being, he can from that moment on no longer stand in humility and gratitude before God. The "death of God," as Nietzsche was well aware and shouted at the top of his voice — though some of his followers today try to avoid saying this too loudly — comes when we are bold enough to decide to "kill" the divinity who exists over against ourselves, the presence who challenges our entire independence.

Thus we find that Tillich believed the word "God" to be a symbol for our awareness of the ultimate. He explained that all symbols die, and that the word "God" also may die. But in that event we can hang on, momentarily though not indefinitely, to an immediate awareness of the absolute reality that continues to be even when "God" seems to have been swallowed up in the abyss of doubt. We can be sure of the "God above God." This "God above God" is guaranteed in Tillich's thought by his static metaphysic of Being; but once a dynamic metaphysic takes over this certainty disappears too.

144

Instead of a Tillich's "courage to be" we require a courage to do without God for a whole lifetime (which Tillich thought impossible), and that means a courage undertaking to "kill" God. Our awareness of the divine now must no longer depend on finding symbols outside ourselves that will point us towards the divine. Our own being henceforth must be all we need. Therefore the Christian atheists ask us either to plunge into the present and immerse ourselves wholly there (Altizer) or else live in hope, without regret spoiling our present optimistic temper (William Hamilton).

How the New Theologies lead logically to the idea of the "death" of God in order to permit the freedom of man may be seen in Harvey Cox's comments on Christian atheism. Reading *The Secular City*, with its many appeals to "biblical theology," its references to the God who guided Israel and revealed himself in Jesus, we might imagine that this thinker, even if he has doubts about being able to name God now, must believe in a fully living God. Yet it is clear that he too, when the chips are down, wills the death of God. In an essay "The Death of God and the Future of Theology," published in an anthology *The New Christianity* (ed. William R. Miller, 1967), he writes:

> The "death-of-God syndrome" signals the collapse of the static order and fixed categories by which men have understood themselves in the past. It opens the future in a new and radical way. . . . [The community of faith] . . . must clarify the life-and death options open to *homo sapiens*, devote itself unsparingly to the humanization of city and cosmos, and keep alive the hope of a kingdom of racial equality, peace among the nations and bread for all. One should never weep for a dead god. A god who can die deserves no tears. Rather we should rejoice that, freed of another incubus, we now take up the task of fashioning a future made possible not by anything that "is" but by "He who comes" (pp. 388f.; also in *On Not Leaving It to the Snake*, pp. 12-13).

From this illuminating comment we may safely draw at least three conclusions. First, that since statements about God are bound up with man's understanding of himself, the word "God" for Cox signifies the Absolute of a metaphysic, the shape of a world-view. To say that God "has died in our generation," then, signifies the breakdown of a metaphysic of Being ("fixed

145

categories") and points to the need for a metaphysic of Becoming in order to view the universe as a process of unfolding meaning. God *is* a metaphysical entity, only this entity, being a process, can be described specifically only as a final end: nothing that "is," something that "comes." Second, the Church or community of faith is *homo sapiens* religiously organized to look after the needs of *homo sapiens,* proving that man does not live by bread alone, but by the faith that tells him he lives by bread alone. Third, the God outside ourselves has been an "incubus," one before whom we ought never to have stood, since he oppressed us. We created him out of a false metaphysic. To these three conclusions from the theories Cox asks us to assent to, I think a fourth ought to be added, although he does not suggest it even indirectly. This is, if we cannot weep for a God who has died, we would be unwise to cheer for a God who succeeds this dead God. A God who can pick up where a dead God has left off is not himself likely to live very long. It would surely be rather simple-minded of us to expect the arrival of a nameless God who is coming, like Santa Claus, with his bag full of goodies for those who behave properly. Perhaps, like Linus of Charles Schulz's admirable comic strip, Cox is telling us that the Great Pumpkin is sure to come, if we wait in a *sincere* pumpkin patch, that is, among the community of believers in process rather than in fixed categories.

If man has really come of age, then surely he should have better things to do than to kill off old God-hypotheses and to propose new ones; particularly when the "theology" that justifies the activity seems to establish nothing except the opinions of those who have no interest in God-talk of any sort, and to whom the announcement that God is dead means no more than a quaint piece of poetic nonsense — since they never have given a thought to his being alive. We would all like to live in a "kingdom" free from race riots, involvement in foreign wars, and poverty. But not too many people actually live in a literal kingdom any more, and few surely could be persuaded to call their country a kingdom because of a hypothetical God who is said to be coming some day. The advocates of secular Christianity believe that this vision is the contemporary form of Christianity because it is the form of faith to which our age can genuinely respond. It is "new," and therefore exciting; whereas any form of supernaturalism is old, and raises only apathetic disbelief.

I doubt it. Supernaturalism, or any form of Christianity, is not a popular creed today. But a refurbished liberalism, sanctifying "secular" existence, is inherently unexciting, for it resembles a proposal to increase the efficiency of our automobiles by adding a fifth wheel. Furthermore, I believe that the call to deify process and progress, and to "rejoice" in leaving behind a dead God, is understood by an increasing number of people to be no gospel but a wholly sinister invitation.

Northrop Frye in *The Modern Century* (1967) has reviewed the way in which the rise of modern technology started by exhilarating us and has recently begun to scare us. He writes:

> The prestige of the myth of progress developed a number of value-assumptions: the dynamic is better than the static, process better than product, the organic and vital better than the mechanical and fixed, and so on. We still have these assumptions, and no doubt they are useful, though like other assumptions we should be aware that we have them. And yet there was an underlying tendency to alienation in the conception of progress itself. In swift movement we are dependent on a vehicle and not on ourselves, and the proportion of exhilaration to apprehensiveness depends on whether we are driving it or merely riding in it. All progressive machines turn out to be things ridden in, with an unknown driver (p. 31).

Hence, says Frye, we have become more and more convinced that the goal of the modern world is more likely to be a disaster than an improvement. Moreover, progress makes us vividly aware of the passage of time. But the individual is not progressing to anything certain except his own death; and so, as the center of our attention becomes fixed on the future, we face with ever-increasing anxiety a future of dread and uncertainty, ending in the certainty of extinction.

At the present stage in our human experience news of a God who is not the product of our self-understanding, but the one before whom we are always standing, comes, *pace* Cox, as more than an echo of a collapsed static order. This God, who is "spirit" and belongs to another order than that of our "fleshly" existence, is no more believable or unbelievable than he always was. Unknown by the "natural" man, he is ever living to faith. And in days when the polyphony of life to which Bonhoeffer referred is so largely unheard, drowned out by the noise of the secular city, with its internal hatreds and its external warfare, the man of today can understand the necessity for a *cantus firmus,* even if he thinks it to be beyond his powers to find a wholeness that it could give.

Here conservative theology emerges as a real option. For the conservatives have never retreated from belief in the uniqueness of the gospel or the authority of the biblical message. They have always maintained that God's Word to man is an objective certainty reaching man with an assurance of hope and wholeness in total contrast to all the brittle human schemes of self-salvation. They can point to the great body of traditional theology, so rational and so constructive in contrast to the short-lived fashions in present-day thinking, where iconoclastic programs win an ephemeral success and then vanish into oblivion. And they can urge that the old, old story of salvation by Jesus Christ has not lost meaning for modern man, since thousands still respond to the story faithfully preached, finding in the reality of transformed lives that the power of the living God is as much at work today as ever.

All this is true. Yet it remains true also that Christian conservatism lives from the work of thinkers in the past who wrestled with what it meant to be a Christian in their times. Their language and their concepts were produced in the context of their age, and however permanently useful their formulations are, we are shirking our duty if we fail to be as adventurous in our thinking as they were, or if we refuse to take our own day as seriously as they took theirs. We can hardly avoid seeing that the sphere of faith of conservative Christianity has shrunk almost entirely to the purely personal dimension of life, and that, though the will to extend the fruits of faith to the social field is certainly present, its practical application goes little beyond pointing to former standards of social righteousness and demanding faithfulness to these. Perhaps the best indication of the inadequacy of conservatism as a live option today is the revolution now going on in the Church of Rome. There the "thaw" following Vatican II has rocked the most conservative institution existing in the contemporary world.

Even a partial relaxation of the formerly rigid rule that kept the whole communion bound to follow obediently the authoritarian discipline of the ecclesiastical hierarchy has produced an explosive situation causing grave concern even among the "liberals" who worked most strenuously to achieve the change. It is not merely a few vociferous rebels but also some highly respected theologians who have either left their Church, believing it to be hopelessly outmoded, or are protesting from within that reform must be far more radically pursued if it is to have any effect at all. The consensus of the "liberals" — most of whom would be considered extremely conservative theologically by Protestant liberals — seems to be that the modern world has moved on to a point where the thinking of the Church (to say nothing of its practice) has lost contact with it.

It is possible, surely, to live in faith as a contemporary person without putting back the clock, refusing to reckon with the realities of the twentieth century, or retreating into a "conservative reconstruction" of purely personal piety. I believe that Bonhoeffer has suggested a way with his understanding of the "natural" and life in the "penultimate" and "ultimate" spheres; though, of course, our situation has changed since his lifetime and requires new adventurings and new perspectives.

THIRTEEN

RELIGION AND MAN'S COMING OF AGE

TWO STATEMENTS AND ONE COMMENT

It matters not how strait the gate,
How charged with punishments the scroll,
I am the master of my fate;
I am the captain of my soul.
— from "Invictus," by W. E. Henley

But as I raved and grew more wild
At every word,
Methought I heard one calling 'Child';
And I replied, 'My Lord.'
— from "The Collar," by George Herbert

"You see, my dear, it is only the big men
who can be treated as children."
— Andrew Undershaft in Major Barbara
by George Bernard Shaw

The concept of "religion" that Bonhoeffer learned from Barth is one that may yet be decisive, more almost than anything else, for permitting us to find order in the midst of the present confusions about the contemporary understanding of Christian faith.

If the conservative approach to Christianity seems to "put back the clock," this is chiefly because conservatives ask us to accept more than just the historic Christian faith that we cannot disregard if we are in honesty to call ourselves Christians. They ask us to accept also the intellectual forms in which the faith has come down to us in the conservative church bodies from the eighteenth and nineteenth centuries. In other words, they wish to preserve intact the religious garment that has clothed the gospel hitherto. It is interesting that Bonhoeffer, when he explained what he meant by "religion," answered, first "metaphysics" and second "individualism" or "methodism." I have argued that "metaphysics" is what liberal Protestantism has stood for, explicitly or implicitly. I would suggest in addition that "individualism" or an individualistic pietism, which is what Bonhoeffer seems to mean by *methodism,* is what conservative Protestantism has stood for.

To find a way to a faith that keeps continuity with the historic Christian gospel, yet engages with present-day existence, then, we ought to start by asking what place "religion" ought to occupy in our thinking about faith and its communication. If Bonhoeffer, as I believe, was wrong in thinking that religion could be completely abandoned, and if his practice in fact contradicted his theory as far as religious observances were concerned, there is justification for believing that a fresh approach to the question of relating religion to faith in our age may be fruitful. I believe that this can be done by using Bonhoeffer's category, set out in the *Ethics,* of "the natural" as the "penultimate." The reason for thinking that this category is particularly relevant to the modern scene is that it may help us to see how "man come of age" still needs religion, but need not be bound by it as an ultimate that comes between him and faith. While it is true now, as it has been in the past, that faith does not become available for us without the "garment" of religion, yet perhaps for the first time in our day our perception of the world allows us to distinguish between the garment and "the thing itself" much more readily than in the past.

Starting with "the natural" means that we can admit the portion of insight contained in the theory of secular Christianity. That is, men today have learned that life can be good and creative in this earth apart from religion. The secular, as well as the sacred, gives scope to a satisfying life. They have therefore gone on to draw a further conclusion. The secular, they decide, is the sphere where everyone is concerned, since everyone must eat, find shelter, and maintain himself against non-human and human enemies. Concern for the sacred, resulting in being religiously minded, is all right for those who want it, but it is obviously an optional extra to "real" living. So secularism is born, the secular city canalizes the energies of society, and those who wish to "clear a space for religion in the world" raise the cry that to be really religious is to be religiously zealous in the service of the secular.

The concept of the natural, on the other hand, recognizes that "real" living is living in relation to God, our Creator and Redeemer. This is life in the "spirit." Worldly life concentrates on living in the natural world, which is the world men must live in as human beings, and is first in their human scale of priorities because human beings are "flesh." God made us in his own image so that we could know him and praise him. But he also made us beings fitted to live in the same world as plants and animals, so that we could enjoy our worldly life. Our environment and skill to adapt ourselves to it were his gifts to us.

Thus, whereas the sacred and the secular are rivals — one of which is likely to destroy the other, since both are "fleshly" concerns — enjoyment of the natural is not in opposition to the service of God, and in an unfallen world would have developed in harmony with it. When God makes us free in Christ he frees us also in the world, not *for* the world but for a richer life in nature and in society.

Once the "natural" is substituted for the "secular" we are rid of the dilemma of having to choose to live either in the secular or in the sacred, so that the secular world becomes either totally a world of skepticism or a world of the "flesh" forced to carry the value of "spirit" and so to be a this-worldly, idolatrous religion. From this other perspective, the natural looks to a world beyond itself; it is the "penultimate" to the "ultimate" (or in traditional terminology "the supernatural"). Love and concern for our neighbor then become our duty and our privilege. Instead of a good work that is an end in itself, our service in the natural is the expression of our gratitude to Christ, who loves us not for what we are and are able to do, but because he has done for us what we cannot do for ourselves — given us the forgiveness we have not deserved. Service lies under the luminous shadow of the cross, instead of being demanded by a God who will emerge when the world-process is complete.

Secularism always treats the world around us simply as the raw material out of which the City of Man is to be built. Having desacralized nature, it has no respect for the natural order but seeks to subdue it ever more thoroughly and to wring from it all that is needed — or wanted even if not needed — to satisfy the insatiable appetites of its masters. This inhumanity of the secular world has often been described and decried, but the complaint is usually dismissed as romantic sentimentality and a foolish desire to return to the simpler conditions of a rural or village economy. Yet secular disregard for the worth of nature in itself and apart from its utility to man has its effect in a corresponding lack of respect for the human life it seeks to improve and humanize. The secular city does make life more comfortable and rewarding for many, but at the same time it spreads both misery and frustration and increasingly regiments the citizens whom it promises to liberate.

This will not surprise the Christian who acknowledges the fallenness of the natural life, a condition that makes inevitable an existence which is unnatural as well as replete with natural good. The earth is always, as Bonhoeffer never wearied of saying, both under the mercy and the judgment of God. The sun still shines on the just and the unjust, even if it shines through city smog. And, of course, technopolis provides — for some — more opportunity than in previous times to rise above the smog in air-conditioned jets and escape for a few days to some "unspoiled" location.

What we need, in order to realize our full humanity, to truly come of age, is a resacralization of the earth; not, of course, a return to pagan beliefs in localized deities or to any variety of pantheism, but to a recognition that God's creation reflects the glory of its Creator. We live in a fallen world, and we do not see it as God saw it when he pronounced it good. Yet that goodness is still there. And, though man has been empowered to subdue the earth, the earth is not only good *for him;* it is good in its own right, for it was pronounced good before man came. We ought to cultivate, therefore, a *consciously religious* attitude to the world, including man's world of art, science, and technology, and the City of Man itself.

153

The necessary word here is "conscious." Bonhoeffer wished to see the end of religion because religion for him was an impediment to our believing reception of the revelation of the one true God, the God of Jesus Christ. In choosing to be religious we were, he believed, choosing idolatry. So in these circumstances the rise of secular society performed a salutary work in showing man that he did not have to be religious. A religionless world freed man to acknowledge the God before whom we are always standing, because it destroyed man-made idols. The choice was choice between clearing a space in this world for religion or of worshipping the God who was not of this world, but its Creator. Secular men, nevertheless, were certain that nothing except this world had reality, and they cleared the ground of divinities in order to leave room for no rival faith to self-worship.

The theory of secular Christianity stemming from Gogarten has tried to distinguish between *secularity,* the product of Christian belief in the goodness of this world, and *secularism,* an idolatrous ideology. But the mistake here is in conceiving the "secular" as having any possible meaning except in relation to the "sacred." Christianity does not lead to a secular theology but to a theology of the natural. Secularity is simply secularism not yet certain of its power to crush the sacred and take over its function. The biblical view is that man has been given delegated power over the natural world. Yet the natural world never exists solely for man, and certainly not for autonomous man. It exists both to show the glory of God and to serve the good of man who knows how to praise God for his good gifts.

The truth embedded in the idea of a secular Christianity and there distorted, is that God does not intend man to live always and only in the sacred, always turning to his Maker and consciously praising him, but also in the secular, simply enjoying his Maker's gifts because they are good. The natural world is good for man, if never only for man. This is what makes it possible for man to clear a space for religion in the world for another purpose than that of worshipping either the world or his own world-view as though these were God. In relation to the world, there is a healthy, non-idolatrous religion, lacking which man lives a less than fully human life. This religion is, to use an old name, *natural piety.*

Natural piety stands for the world resacralized yet not redivinized. It is a conscious recognition that we did not create the world. Therefore the world, both the sphere we call nature, and the sphere of human productivity that shapes nature for human purposes, has more than an instrumental value. Today we all recognize the fact, stated so well by Northrop Frye, that the secular city, the sphere acknowledging human purposes alone and constructed primarily to achieve human good, is becoming steadily more inhuman, more impersonal, and more destructive of personality at the same time as it seeks — to some extent successfully — to enlarge and extend man's freedom from the limitations of nature. We still can live creative human lives; yet it is often in spite of, rather than because of, the existence of the secular city. And frequently our enjoyment of life's good things feels like the distraction of playing a game of cards in a railway car that is hurtling on to the edge of a yawning chasm. Natural piety, consciously cultivated, gives us an alternative fashion of living our lives.

Natural piety, as the poet Wordsworth once said, yields a vision of existence that allows us to see our life "tied day to day." The present concern over the meaninglessness of life — which is much more than the concern of existentialists and their friends, as Cox would try to persuade us — comes from the inability to see life as anything more than a futile piling up of hours or a boring routine. Our humorous references to the "rat race" are attempts to hide from ourselves the features of despair in the face of our technological society. Natural piety means the cultivation of a rhythm of ordinary life, largely through the observance of symbolic acts or ceremonies which humanize routine. Many of these human ceremonies linger on today as peremptory conventions — the handshake is the most obvious of these, and the family meal is probably the most "meaningful" (the best preserved). Natural piety is thus a human religion. It does not seek to worship any deity, but to give ordinary existence a fixed and dependable worth, consecrated by means of an accepted ritual. It uses the God-given power of the creative imagination, the human ability to form symbols in order to unite the scattered moments of our experience, that the natural world may have a shape and substance in which we may feel at home insofar as the changes of time

155

and space can afford us a welcome resting-place on our pilgrimage through the world. Even the bitterness of death itself,
which nothing on earth can fully take away, is eased by natural piety, which reminds us that bodily death is a sleep, and to
the tired frame of man may come as a welcome friend.

Natural piety is most easily seen to be a human activity
fully belonging to the natural sphere; it is thus not an idolatrous, substitute faith but a means of expressing faith in God's
continual love of his world insofar as it is his good creation.
What applies to natural piety may be extended also to religion
in all its aspects where these are kept from being engulfed in
man's presumptuous self-worship. Bonhoeffer himself shows how
the ritual of the Christian Year — a *religious* creation if ever
there was one — became for him a genuine means of grace.
Instead of finding his prison life *merely* what he often knew
it to be *also,* a monotonous round of empty days punctuated
by periods of apparently random terror when the bombers were
overhead, he spoke of the passing from one feast day to another
which made him remember happy times in the past and wait
in expectation of mercies yet to come. It is certain that his trust
in divine providence, so often referred to in the prison letters,
did not depend upon the markings on the religious calendar.
Yet it is also certain that the calendar of feasts was part of
his human equipment that enabled him to endure when he
might otherwise have broken down. Religion, we may confidently assert, is made for man and not man for religion. So
long as we know that faith is more than a human construct,
however, it would be foolish to pretend that we can live religionless as though we were superhuman beings. Religion is,
humanly speaking, a creation of humanity. At the same time,
as all good things are, it is finally a gift of God and shaped
by him to save us from ourselves; and, as all good things may
be, it may be turned into a monstrous evil by our pride or
stupidity when we forget that God alone merits our supreme
loyalty.

What is true of religion as ritual and sacred observance is
also true of our religious concepts and picturings. The whole
muddle that Robinson has led his readers into by talking about
the impossibility of keeping today the image of a God "up
there" or "out there" has its origin in a failure to make clear

from the first the God he was trying to find an image for. Of course, if our belief is in a God who is an extension of our being, then the image of a God "in the depths" will be appropriate. If, on the other hand, we are concerned to find a suitable image for a God who is *other* than we are, who is "spirit" and not "flesh," then either "up there" or "out there" will do very well. Few of us are naive literalists believing that when prices go up all the goods in the supermarket have to be picked off the ceiling, or that in order to look down on our neighbor we have to be taller than he is. Why need we waste a moment over explaining images that are employed because they are more immediately understandable than explanations? Also, the possible use of the metaphor of depth would cause no problem as *one* metaphor to the believer in a God ordinarily thought of as "outside" us, since the metaphor of "in the depths" is quite proper when speaking of the immanence of the transcendent God. As soon as it is insisted that the metaphor of depth is the sole permissible one, however, we are alerted to the presence of a dogmatic belief in a God who is *only* immanent, or else whose transcendence is limited to his being the absolute extension of our inner consciousness.

Similarly, the dispute about whether God must be less than God if he is described as *a* Being presents no grave intellectual problem. If we call God a Being, we cannot be thinking of him existing "alongside" other beings as a mountain exists alongside a tortoise. We are thinking of God, after all, the Creator of every "being." The image we are using here is one excluding the notion that God is a part or aspect or dimension of any or all possible beings we know in God's creation. We are asserting that God is complete in himself and independent of the world, just as one created being exists independently from another. The image is nonliteral and a parallel to the image of God being "outside" us. In the latter image we hardly imagine that a strong enough telescope would soon locate God if our unaided eyes did not. The reason we have trouble with images is that we do not trust them to do their job. We do not listen to hear what they are saying, extremely distinctly, in the ear of our imagination; although, every day, we employ thousands of images in ordinary speech, and understand how to use them so well that we never stop to think even that they are images.

Of course, matters become considerably more complex when we enter the arena of philosophical theology. Philosophers generally make extensive use of "stipulative definitions," where words are given a special, restricted meaning for the purpose of more precise explanation. For example, in Leslie Dewart's *The Future of Belief: Theism in a World Come of Age* (1966) it is suggested that we should not speak of God as "a being" but instead refer to his "presence." The context makes clear that Dewart, who is a Roman Catholic and wants to revise traditional language, not to abolish it, by no means denies that God is not "outside" us. Rather, he hopes his suggested terminology will be less misunderstood than the old words and phrases are in the contemporary world. Now, it happens more often than perhaps we realize that a philosopher's technical terms get taken up into common speech because they reflect actual changes that have been taking place in our way of thinking and speaking. Each generation uses words a little differently from its predecessor, and some words change their meaning drastically within quite a short period of time. Perhaps some of Dewart's suggestions will be adopted in the future: time will tell. Yet we can be fairly certain that a philosopher's suggestion about Christian language will prove permanently useful for Christians only when they reflect the demands of faith.

Dewart pleads for a "dehellenization" of (Catholic) theological language. Insofar as his intent is to free biblical terms from being made captive to Greek philosophical thinking most Christians (especially Protestant ones!) will say "Amen." But he also seems to wish to change Christian language in order to encourage an approach to God that is at least as much a product of a very limited "contemporary" viewpoint as it is of biblical study. Thus, after saying that we should speak about the God of grace rather than about the God of the Greeks who is a First Cause (p. 206), he goes on to suggest that God is "a friendly and benevolent pervasive presence in every reality which ... should normally produce the Christian's appreciation of existence, his enjoyment of life, and the consequent moral obligation of charity towards our fellow man" (p.

207). Such a description indeed speaks of God's grace and mercy. It conspicuously does not speak of the biblical stress upon God as the consuming fire, upon the God who brings his mercy *and his judgment* to bear upon all human endeavor — even the most well meant and most highly praised among men. Here the prejudice of modernity is at least as evident in Dewart's proposed reconstruction as is fidelity to biblical categories.

It is highly illuminating that Dewart should make the objection that "to attribute existence to God is the most extreme form of anthropomorphism" (p. 180). He evidently assumes that the man of today has outgrown the need for speaking of God in images drawn from human existence. This is an assumption with little basis in reality. Where else do we turn for our images? Every image, of course, may become an idol. We may mistake our poor form of words for the one who is beyond all thought and imagining. Yet the prophets who had most to say about the folly and faithlessness of idolatry were never hesitant to draw upon human life when they described God as Shepherd, Father, Comforter, Lord of Hosts, Holy One of Israel. Have we outgrown altogether their limitations? Not the least conspicuous quality in the writings of those who adopt most enthusiastically the notion of man's coming of age is the note of complacency. They often exhibit a surprising readiness to think that humanity is endlessly to be congratulated upon reaching this exciting stage. No doubt congratulations are in order, but a few warnings as well about the responsibilities of maturity might not come amiss. It is not exactly the mark of being grown-up always to be harping upon the fact. Being adult does not totally alter our personalities or mean that the faults visible in our childhood must suddenly disappear never to emerge again. It is even possible that we may gain a few more vices in addition to those already well established.

Genuine maturity neither takes itself too seriously nor cuts itself off from delight in simple ways. The person who on one occasion reads Ludwig Wittgenstein's *Tractatus Logico-Philosophicus* is likely also on another occasion to turn to *Winnie the Pooh* — and unlikely to leave the Latin translation of A. A. Milne's book lying about conspicuously on the coffee table. There seems to be a widening gulf these days between "popular"

159

books on religious topics and "serious" (or academic) ones. While the duty of being contemporary is declared on every side, the courtesy of writing plainly where this can be done without sacrificing accuracy is all too little practiced when so much theology is written in almost impenetrable jargon. However, this is a minor if not insignificant matter. More important by far is the increasing tendency to forget that theology is, to use Karl Barth's term, a *happy* science. Straining to make their subject intellectually respectable in the eyes of an imagined (and possibly imaginary) "modern man," interpreters of Christianity are apt to lose the simplicity that even the most sophisticated treatment of their subject ought to allow to shine out. After all, God is not only the greatest of mysteries to our intelligence, he is also the best of all companions on life's journey.

Anthropomorphism is a long word. *God* is a very short one — as short as *man* and *sin*. *Faith* and *grace* are short words too. Man come of age has almost certainly not outgrown his need of religion, though human needs are not always consistent through the centuries. Anthropomorphic language about God is a human way to picture "the beyond in the midst" that man shows no sign of outgrowing. For to call God "Father" and "Lord" is not just the most basic method of producing understandable images of God, it is the most natural way of responding to his forgiving love.

FOURTEEN

BOTH THE NEW AND THE OLD

*I will call to mind the deeds of the
        Lord;
    yea, I will remember thy wonders
        of old.
I will meditate on all thy work,
    and muse on thy mighty deeds.
Thy way, O God, is holy.
    What god is great like our God?
Thou art the God who workest
        wonders,
    who hast manifested thy might
        among the peoples.
Thou didst with thy arm redeem
        thy people,
The sons of Jacob and Joseph.*

                                    — Psalm 77:11-15

*Live as free men; not however as though your freedom
were there to provide a screen for wrongdoing, but as
slaves in God's service. Give due honor to everyone:
love to the brotherhood, reverence to God, honor to the
sovereign.*

                                    — I Peter 2:16-17

At the beginning of this survey of New Theology, I spoke
first about the overvaluation of newness in our society, and
second about our present consciousness of a generation gap
preventing free communication between different age groups.

It seems fitting now to return to these themes before closing the record.

The overvaluation of newness that comes from taking technological progress to be the model of all life has plainly affected our thinking about Christianity. We are almost getting to the point where we wait to see what the style of this year's religious thinking is going to be, much as we wait to see the new styling of this year's automobiles. In both instances, we may experience a sense of letdown if, after all, no very radical change of style is forthcoming.

Such a comparison is not too farfetched, either. I notice that the phrase "theological style" is popular, while the phrase "religious philosophy of life" has vanished from the face of the earth. Yet, a glance at the religious literature produced when our century was young shows that nearly every book claiming to be progressive was then urging its readers to adopt "a new religious philosophy that has cast off for ever the outworn dogmas of the past, a philosophy fully acceptable to the modern mind." *Then,* it was assumed that a new religious philosophy, like a good new watch, would last a lifetime. *Now,* if we do not keep looking out of the window, we may be caught with an old-style "theology" and all the embarrassment that follows from not having realized that pessimistic Christian existentialism is "out" and optimistic secular Christianity is "in" — or *vice versa.*

Yet the proliferation of new religious programs under the New Theology umbrella is not, in itself, anything to worry about unduly. We belong to a big, untidy civilization in which we are accustomed to a thousand voices daily exhorting us to buy, to boycott, to join, to jeer, to vote, to veto, to sign, to sing, to think for the sake of efficiency, to march for the sake of others, and to drop out for the sake of ourselves. Being stirred up by a lot of people shouting contradictory advice may be at the moment a salutary experience for the Church. What ought to cause us real concern are the long-term effects of believing the new in the area of faith to be as vital as the new in the area of technology. To some it seems a real proof of Christianity's being still in business that it is able to launch a new slogan into the stratosphere of the mass media almost as often as Cape Kennedy launches its rockets. Ultimately, confusion about what the Christian faith is and how it is to be interpreted must result in public apathy and private despair. It may be exhilarating for a short time to cry that we are free to proclaim the death of God or to elect ourselves to the position of being God's *avant-garde* in the secular city. Very soon we will realize that the only slogan left is "You shall surely die." Meanwhile, the secular city will continue to exhibit complete indifference as to whether we are sharing in its triumphs or disasters.

The fact that life cannot be assimilated to the progressive pattern of technology is brought home to us in the so-called "crisis in communication." An age that finds it less and less possible to communicate worthwhile ideas, that depends upon ready-made entertainment, and that runs to illusion-creating drugs in search of a personal, human vision in the midst of an impersonal, dehumanizing order, has responded gratefully to the slogan "the Medium is the Message." This slogan allows us to feel that we need not bother about the triviality of the television programs provided for us by the incomprehensible wisdom of the secular city (which graciously tells us we are getting what we really want), because we are participating in a truly contemporary experience. The catch is that the combined message of all the media seems to be, "Eat, drink, and like it, for tomorrow you die. You can travel now, or go on a trip, and pay later. It is later, though, than you think."

Secularity, and not just secularism, overrates newness and dreams of life as continuously progressing. When we wake up from the secular dream and look at the reality of life confronting us, however, we see that the next step for humanity seems to leave us the bitter choice between chaos or regimentation; and either way humanity loses. It is religion, pointing to a wholeness beyond the flux of time and a reality beyond the inevitability of death, that alone offers the possibility of keeping life in the human dimension. If our sole religion is the worship of humanity, then our man-made God will turn out to be an inhuman monster, a demon preserving his own life by devouring his children. Happily, we have not yet become completely committed to the secular. Both in our social and our individual existence we still remember and partly live by religious values, including Christian ones. We have not sold ourselves irrevocably to death. We continue to live in community with the living past and not wholly in the atomistic, secular present.

Religion's perennial function is to keep the new, which is essential for ongoing life, from being parted from the old, which is essential for passing on the values painfully gained by man in his long history. A man who has lost his memory beyond recall cannot last as a human being; and religion is the memory-preserving element in the life of humanity.

In this connection, Bishop Pike's definition of a Christian in *A Time for Christian Candor* (p. 63) as one who remembers the death and resurrection of Christ is, in principle, correct. Yet Pike is so concerned to tell us all the things a Christian today need *not* remember that he leaves us with the impression that his Christianity is a rather arbitrary and sterile affair. A Christian remembers the death and resurrection of Christ above all; yet he remembers also the whole biblical story explaining the person and the work of Christ, and remembers too the story of the Christian Church that brings him into living relationship with the living Lord today and sets him in the midst of the communion of saints. Anything suggesting that he can break, without serious consequences, the links binding him to the Christian past or to other Christians threatens the integrity of his religious life and sets him on the quest for a new and more satisfying religion.

For a long time it was thought that the word "religion" came from the Latin verb "to bind" *(religare)*. It is more likely that it comes from the verb "to care for" or "to give heed to" *(religere)*. Both explanations add up to much the same thing. The person giving heed to the divine is the person who acknowledges an obligation (a "binding") to that which is beyond his own personal existence. He acknowledges a law other than his own wishes, a truth other than his own experience, standards other than current opinion. The secular man, on the other hand, being the person who does not care about the transcendent, is not bound to care for anything beyond his immediate interests. He may, perhaps, decide to care for others out of a sense of social solidarity (the ethical man). But, equally, he may be one who "couldn't care less." This is why, in the sphere of conduct, the religious man is concerned more with preserving firm standards of morality than with the personal happiness of individuals. To obey the will of God is for him more important than to find immediate personal development. He believes that enduring happiness lies in the way of obedience to the Lord in whose service is perfect freedom.

Religion is not the same as faith. In emphasizing this, both Barth and Bonhoeffer rightly noted that the atheistic protest against the evils brought by religion is one that the Christian must readily agree to be correct. Christian religion itself has often been a heavy burden laid on the shoulders of mankind, and the secular denial of the right of religious authority to control community existence is fully justified.

In countless ways, the pluralistic culture in which we live is greatly to be preferred to the old ideal of "Christian civilization," which in actual fact meant ecclesiastical dictatorship. Yet the so-called secular culture that has succeeded the medieval and the Reformation religious establishments has not meant the advent of sweetness and light. If the numbers of innocent people killed, tortured, and allowed to live homeless and without hope are relevant evidence, the new society has been if anything more cruel, more inhuman, and more tyrannical than its predecessors. Since the seventeenth century we can point to splendid advances in humanitarian patterns of existence. And in most of these advances — from the outlawing of legalized torture, through the abolition of slavery, to the present struggle for racial equality — the driving forces in reform have been made up of an odd combination of antireligious humanists and Christians, both liberal and conservative in doctrine.

Today we depend largely upon the hope that there remains enough of the same spirit that activated the champions of reform in the past to move our large-scale City of Man towards choosing life rather than death for us all. At the moment we have no better basis for expecting to continue to exist as a world than the hope-against-hope that no nation will risk world suicide to assert its own will. We have to bank on the supposition, however uncertainly founded, that our leaders will continue to place enlightened self-interest above irrational will-to-power. Meanwhile, in the context of total fear, our individual lives go on. For all the near-miraculous changes technology has brought, man's life still treads the old path between happiness and misery, purposefulness and aimlessness, creativity and sterility. Each day piles up its little heap of profits and losses for each of us, and brings us a step nearer our death.

The contemporary Christian continues to ask what God requires of him each day, both in action and in understanding. And the direction in which the exponents of New Christianity ask us to look for an answer appears to me to be precisely the wrong direction. For they suggest that we must look to the future we are to shape ourselves, to the new that has left the old behind, and to the secular that denies and negates religion. I believe, on the contrary, that Thomas à Kempis' dictum, "man proposes, God disposes," should direct our attitude to the future; and that, if we leave the old behind, the new will either be stillborn or born misshapen. The most urgent requirement of our contemporary culture is to repossess God's good gift of religion, a gift enabling man to lay hold of, enrich, and preserve his humanity.

The history of Western civilization has shown how evil a thing religion can be when it is made the tool of human ambition and lust for power. But the abuse of religion confirms rather than denies its use. Religion is the binding force that preserves the human world from disintegrating into shattered pieces emptied of the harmony, beauty, tranquillity, and utility they possessed when held in unity. Our culture still lives largely from the values in the arts, the sciences, and the ordinary conduct of life that were hammered out during the period when the ideal of "Christendom" was the religious pattern that men strove to make visible in society. Today we are increasingly conscious of the fragmentation of life, both personal and social. We are surrounded by the "problems" caused by broken treaties, broken truces, broken respect for law, broken homes, broken minds, and broken hopes. Physically, the community of man is broken by sealed frontiers; while the inward shattering of unity has now for a long time been the preoccupation of the artist in our midst. Perhaps the most ominous feature of our broken world is the recent breaking out into violence of long-festering resentments, born of frustrated hopes on the part of those who thought the secular city would make them free. While the rioting in the Negro ghettos in the cities of the Northern States is the clearest example of this trend to date, the trend has set in and has limitless scope for development.

I have suggested that a rediscovery of "natural piety" is required to bring our broken culture on to the path of wholeness. It will not solve any of the acute "problems" facing contemporary society, of course, any more than a balanced diet will solve the problem of acute appendicitis, or a happy home life mend a child's broken leg. Natural piety is religion at its most elementary level — and at its most elemental too, it might be said, since it is nature worship freed from idolatry and humanized. It has been well understood by some of our greatest modern scientists, who recognize how the pursuit of truth teaches us humility before the mystery of nature; and, because of its "nonsupernatural" character, it may be able to lead the secularized individual to see the world in a new light. It can open a way for the appreciation of transcendent values, so long neglected and reviled.

The basic element in natural piety is reverence for the world in its widest extent and in every dimension where it touches us. Compared with ourselves and our experience, nature is not only very large and very powerful. She is also very old and very wise. Thus natural piety finds in nature concrete evidence of the continuity between the past and the present. The irrational worship of the new, just because it is new, or of the contemporary, just because it is contemporary, is the idolatrous antireligion that natural piety must first challenge and overthrow. The recovery of reverence for history, and for living tradition, is the human dimension of our relationship with nature. Here the idolatrous antireligion is fanatical worship of the nation and its traditions, expressed in fanatical hatred of actual or imaginary enemies of national unity and leading to "right-wing" reaction and ultimately to totalitarian tyranny. At its most universal, natural piety cherishes the ideal of *humanitas*, the humanness of the human. Yet, because a generalized ideal of "the brotherhood of man" is empty and easily perverted into an idolatry of the secular, the natural expression of the ideal of *humanitas* for a Westerner is devotion to the humane tradition of Western culture, Christian and classical, which lives on, though in a debilitated form, in the Western university insofar as the university communities have not been fragmented into dehumanizing "multiversities."

Natural piety, being the enemy of fragmentation, must oppose not only newness for its own sake but also individualism for its own sake (together with individualism's shadow-twin, collectivism). When, for example, the popular deduction is drawn from a situation ethic that an act is "all right so long as nobody gets hurt," the man of natural piety will ask, "But have you remembered everyone who is concerned in this situation?" Those who may get hurt from decisions made in any situation include both people now dead and people who can never possibly know about the individual situation but who may be affected by it in the future, as well as — a frequently forgotten person — the self who acts and whose total character is strengthened or weakened by every choice made and by every value ignored. The man who owns a loyalty to a specific faith as well as to natural piety will say, naturally, that God is the one who enters first into every situation. For a Christian, wrongdoers are judged on the grounds that "with their own hands they are crucifying the Son of God and making mock of his death" (Heb. 6:6).

Natural piety simply insists that each act of every man involves in principle all mankind, past, present, and to come. We do not have to prove ever that we acted lovingly in our choices (something unprovable anyway). To claim for ourselves an intention of pure goodwill shows lack of humility and indicates probable self-deception. We have to satisfy ourselves every time we act, by using all the intelligence and sensitivity we possess, that our decision will neither offend the dignity of man nor give anyone else an excuse for being inhuman in the future because he saw us act out of self-regard and not out of respect for what we judged to be the right. We may hope to be loving. We can only *be* loving insofar as we have achieved personal integrity. Therefore we must always act on principle, even if our principles are less than perfect and may not even be good.

Natural piety turns to the created world and does not explicitly name the name of God. Yet it cannot live severed entirely from faith in a transcendence "beyond" ourselves. It acknowledges, though it does not address, the Creator. The Christian, indeed, can practice natural piety without ceasing to be a Christian, but he can never restrict himself to this religious level. And, when he wants to express his Christian faith explicitly, he has to do so in one form or another of the Christian religion. Christianity has been transmitted down the centuries *religiously,* that is, through specific patterns of religious beliefs and customs, and it is unrealistic to imagine that this faith could ever survive the complete disintegration of its religious garment.

I have argued (Chapter 8) that the intent of Bonhoeffer's "religionless Christianity" is met once we know that Christian faith is not dependent upon any religious premise, so that we no longer argue *from* the truth of religious hypotheses *to* the truth of Christian revelation. Knowing how un-Christian the Christian religion has been in the past, and still continues to be, we do not place our faith in religion. Freed from religious idolatry, we are now open to see the human use of religion, convinced that the God who can make the wrath of man to praise him (Ps. 76:10) can just as easily use human religion in his work of mercy and salvation. Thus we may follow Bonhoeffer's example rather than his exploratory theories, and find the freedom in which Christ has made us free by not assuming that he addresses us always from the side of the "world" and never from the side of religion.

No religion, including the Christian religion, has ever continued long without renewing itself by borrowing from secular culture and pressing the forms of culture into the service of the sacred. We must expect this to happen now, in the twentieth century, if the Christian religion is to continue to be a leaven in contemporary society. The call for a New Christianity has been in part the result of a realization that for the Church to remain shut in a cultural cocoon of antiquated pattern is to sign its own death warrant. The positive side of the movement going under the title of New Theology and New Morality is the way in which it has gone about making suggestions as to ways in which the Church today must change its "image" — a relic of the past carefully preserved in moth balls — and enter into dialogue with the cultural environment in which it is set, an environment secularistic in character in nearly every area.

Had my survey been geared to the positive side of the New Christianity, it would have contained a good deal more honey and much less gall in its judgments about the ferment now going on in the Church. As it is, my role has been apparently that of the wicked fairy-godmother at the baby princess's christening. Where everyone else has blessed the child and predicted a happy and fortunate future, I have thought it my duty to cast a gloom over the proceedings by foretelling disaster. My explanation, which may not be accepted, is that the child in question is not a fairy-tale princess but a very different creature, namely, a religious philosophy.

This particular religious philosophy seems to me to be well intentioned in its conviction that Christianity must escape from the dead past, but disastrously wrong in imagining that the way to help it to do so is to cut the roots that connect it with its past. To leave the past behind is one thing; but to wish to forget and try to negate it is quite another.

Christianity itself from the beginning has combined the old and the new. It was a revolutionary faith, and as a religion cut its bonds that tied it to the religion out of which it was born. It ceased to be a sect of Judaism, and became the Church instead of the Synagogue. Yet the faith that is set out in the New Testament never turned away from the Old Testament, which indeed for a time continued to be regarded as the Church's sole Holy Scripture. The sons of Abraham continued to be the heroes of the new faith, though seen no longer as they saw themselves, but in the light of the coming of the Christ who by "the new, living way" (Heb. 10:20) had fulfilled the promises contained in the old Law. Jesus said to his followers, "When, therefore, a teacher of the law has become a learner in the kingdom of heaven, he is like a householder who can produce from his store both the new and the old" (Matt. 13:52).

This, I believe, is a parable for our times, and in a sense our commission to preach the gospel in the twentieth century. Culturally, our great mistake today in almost every sphere of life is that we are trying to tear the new from the old. The result is all around us: increasing confusion, alienation, discouragement, apathy, and superficial optimism covering a depth of despair. The secular without the sacred will not satisfy

170

us or heal us. Faith without God will not give us a gospel to proclaim. Love without law will not direct us to our true end. Earth without heaven is the grave of our hopes without an Easter light of resurrection to turn the night of weeping into a morning of joy.

We are human beings, so we need a religion to tie each day in our understanding to each other day. But not just any religion can promise us what Christ has promised us if we have living faith in him. And so, if the Christian religion is to be the means of our encountering Christ "new every morning," we must discover it again and again for ourselves. In 1945, the year he was not to live through to the end, Bonhoeffer wrote a poem on the new year (*Letters and Papers,* pp. 249f.), which ends:

> *While all the powers of Good aid and attend us*
> *boldly we'll face the future, be it what may.*
> *At even, and at morn, God will befriend us,*
> *and oh, most surely on each new year's day.*

That is the expression of a religion of genuinely human quality, simple, humble, and unafraid. It is also the expression of faith in one who said, "Behold, I am making all things new." Only because Christians remember that Jesus died and rose again in the old times, almost two thousand years ago, can they be sure he will befriend us today and for ever, and that he is still making all things new.

171

APPENDIX

John A. T. Robinson's *Exploration Into God*
(Stanford, California: Stanford University Press, 1967)

In his most recent book, an expanded version of lectures given in 1966 at Stanford University, California, Bishop Robinson says he has tried "digging deeper" into the question of speaking about God for the modern age than was possible in *Honest To God*. Thus *Exploration Into God* raises high hopes of finding a full clarification of Robinson's view of the God who speaks to us in the Christian revelation.

As in *Honest To God*, Robinson begins with his conviction that there is "a crisis in theism, that is, in the traditional case for belief in the existence of a personal God" (p. 25). He continues:

> The reality that theism sought to safeguard and enshrine is not at issue, nor has it changed — the reality of the God-relationship as utterly personal and utterly central.... The immediate question is how that intensely personal, experienced reality can be represented and given expression in a view of the universe that truly makes it central (p. 26).

This way of stating the issue is pursued throughout the book, and it follows the line of thinking that I have pointed out in connection with Robinson's earlier writings. It assumes that the question of speaking about God is, above all, that of relating our "image" of God to a world-view. The hypothesis of God is to "make sense" in our picturing of the universe. If we can find no use for God in the universe as we conceive it to be, then God simply disappears from sight. Following C. A. van Peursen's analysis of three periods of man's understanding of the universe, the "mythical," the "ontological," and the "functional" — a view, incidentally, strongly reminiscent of Comte's three periods — Robinson concludes that today's way of establishing the reality of God is "to show how he 'comes in,' how he 'works' — in the process of nature and history, rather than behind them or between them. . . . Unless we can represent him in functional rather than ontological terms, he will rapidly lose all reality. As a Being he has no future" (p. 35).

This is allowing the world to dictate the space God must occupy in the world, and allowing it in the most supine way. A theory of human understanding is posited, and immediately God has no future unless he conforms to the expectations of the theory! God is permitted to work alone in the process of nature and history, and nowhere else. He has been put in his place. Obedient to the dictates of this theory, Robinson concludes that the "projection" of the God-image required for the contemporary world is that of *panentheism*. No longer will we speak of God *and* the world. A better analogy will be to speak of the God-world relationship in terms of "the divine field." He explains:

> Instead of postulating a necessary Being for whom the world might or might not exist, we have to begin from the sheer givenness, the isness of the only reality we can certainly know. . . . All statements about God, if we make them, are interpretations of this reality (p. 101).

The only reality we can certainly know. Bonhoeffer insisted that the path of theology goes from God to reality, never from reality to God. Robinson, faithful to the liberal tradition, assumes the opposite. The result, not very surprisingly, is that all Robinson's descriptions of God gravitate to the impersonal, in spite of his protestation that the God-relationship is "utterly personal." No other outcome than making God into an "it" is possible, however, when relationship is made into an ultimate category. Relationship, after all, is a general idea; and it is *the existence of persons* and nothing else that constitutes the personal. Once relationship is allowed primacy over the person, then persons become epiphenomena of an impersonal process. In a remarkable passage Robinson paraphrases the prologue to John's Gospel entirely in impersonal terms, in terms of "it," though apparently without noticing what he has done. "The clue to the universe, as personal," he writes, "was present from the beginning. It was to be found at the level of reality which we call God. Indeed it was no other than God nor God than it" (p. 104).

What is lost in such a paraphrase is the core of the Christian gospel, the concrete message concerning the God who called Abraham and sent Jesus Christ into the world. In place of the utterly personal God appears an abstraction called the "divine personal principle." And in place of the God-man Jesus Christ appears an example of humanity (or, more exactly, the archetypal humanity-figure of Schleiermacher), a general idea manifest briefly in the phenomenal world.

> And this divine personal principle found embodiment in a man and took habitation in our midst. We saw its full glory, in all its utterly gracious reality — the wonderful sight of a person living in uniquely normal relationship to God, as son to father (p. 104).

Jesus lets us see an "it" (in odd combination, a "gracious" it), embodied as a Platonic idea is embodied in spatio-temporal actuality.

In *Honest To God* Robinson declared that "popular supranaturalistic Christology has always been dominantly docetic. That is to say, Christ only appeared to be a man or looked like a man: 'underneath' he was God" (p. 65). This charge is a common one in liberal theology (it was made by Schleiermacher too), yet it is tendentious in face of the traditional "supranaturalistic" insistence that Christ is both God and man. Quite specifically, Robinson's alternative is fully and consistently docetic. In *Honest To God* Christ is said "to be more than just a man: here was a window into God at work" (p. 71). In other words, Christ's God-manhood is not the revelation of God. We have to look *through* the man Jesus Christ in order to see God at work. And in *Exploration Into God* we have to look past the "embodiment" in order to discover the personal principle here embodied. The "body" is inessential. The "principle" is what brings illumination. We have to use the man as a clue to grasp the "reality" of the relationship.

So God, explored by Bishop Robinson, ceases to be the Father, Son, and Spirit of Christian faith, and emerges as a reality-principle.

BIBLIOGRAPHY

Altizer, Thomas J. J. (ed.). *Toward a New Christianity: Readings in the Death of God Theology*. New York: Harcourt, 1967.

Bonhoeffer, Dietrich. *Ethics*. London: SCM, 1955.

———. *Letters and Papers from Prison*. New York: Macmillan, 1962.

Callahan, Daniel (ed.). *The Secular City Debate*. New York: Macmillan, 1966.

Cox, Harvey. *The Secular City: Secularization and Urbanization in Theological Perspective*. Rev. ed. New York: Macmillan, 1966.

Dewart, Leslie. *The Future of Belief: Theism in a World Come of Age*. New York: Herder & Herder, 1966.

Fletcher, Joseph. *Situation Ethics: The New Morality*. Philadelphia: Westminster, 1966.

Frye, Northrop. *The Modern Century*. Toronto: Oxford, 1967.

Koenker, Ernest B. *Secular Salvations*. Philadelphia: Fortress Press, 1965.

Mehta, Ved. *The New Theologian*. New York: Harper, 1965.

Miller, William Robert (ed.). *The New Christianity: An Anthology of the Rise of Modern Religious Thought*. New York: Delacorte, 1967.

Ogden, Schubert M. *The Reality of God and Other Essays*. New York: Harper, 1966.

Peerman, Dean (ed.). *Frontline Theology*. Richmond: John Knox, 1967.

Pelz, Werner and Lotte. *God Is No More*. Philadelphia: Lippincott, 1964.

Pike, James A. *A Time for Christian Candor*. New York: Harper, 1964.

Robinson, John A. T. *But That I Can't Believe*. New York: New American Library, 1967.

———. *Honest To God*. Philadelphia: Westminster, 1963.

——— and David L. Edwards (eds.). *The Honest To God Debate*. Philadelphia: Westminster, 1963.

Tillich, Paul. *The Future of Religions*. New York: Harper, 1966.

van Buren, Paul. *The Secular Meaning of the Gospel Based on an Analysis of its Language*. New York: Macmillan, 1963.

SUGGESTIONS FOR FURTHER READING

Barnette, Henlee H. *The New Theology and Morality*. Philadelphia: Westminster, 1967.

Bolt, David. *Of Heaven and Hope*. New York: John Day, 1965.

Bowden, John and James Richmond. *A Reader in Contemporary Theology*. Philadelphia: Westminster, 1967.

Bruce, Michael. *No Empty Creed*. New York: Seabury, 1966.

Hordern, William. *A Layman's Guide to Protestant Theology*. Rev. ed. New York: Macmillan, 1968.

Jenkins, David. *The Glory of Man*. New York: Scribner's, 1967.

Mascall, E. L. *The Secularisation of Christianity: An Analysis and Critique*. London: Darton, Longman & Todd, 1965.

Morrison, John M. *Honesty and God*. Edinburgh: The Saint Andrew Press, 1966.

Redding, David A. *The New Immorality*. Westwood, N. J.: Revell, 1967.

Richardson, Alan. *Religion in Contemporary Debate*. Philadelphia: Westminster, 1966.

Simon, Ulrich. *Theology Observed*. London: Epworth, 1966.

Vahanian, Gabriel. *No Other God*. New York: George Braziller, 1966.

Vogel, Arthur A. *The Next Christian Epoch*. New York: Harper, 1966.